HOME
TRUTHS
FROM
ABROAD

HOME TRUTHS FROM ABROAD

CHRIS BROAD

with Patrick Murphy

ARTHUR BARKER

an imprint of
George Weidenfeld and Nicolson Limited
London

Published in Great Britain by
George Weidenfeld & Nicolson Limited
91 Clapham High Street
London SW4 7TA

ISBN 0 213 16952 5

Printed in Great Britain by
Butler & Tanner Ltd, Frome and London

Contents

Acknowledgements

Compiling this book has been an enjoyable experience for me and my sincerest thanks go to Pat Murphy for making the task as easy as possible by his organization, turn of speed and admirable knowledge of and insight into cricket as a profession.

I owe a large debt to Reg Sinfield, my longest serving (and long-suffering) coach and critic, whose love of cricket rubbed off so early in my life.

Thanks also to David Graveney, for allowing me to use extracts from his personal letters; to all the snap-happy photographers, for supplying the cricket photographs; to Alfa Romeo, for acknowledging my International Cricketer of the Year award in this country with easily the best car I've ever driven; and to Duncan Fearnley, for the hours of personal attention and degree of perfectionism in making my cricket equipment.

Finally, I am a 'team' man, and I owe a big thank you to my family, Carole's family and our friends for their support and inspiration for both my career and book – thanks Carole, for hoarding every clipping, letter and diary from the last ten years!

Illustrations

Illustrations

Between pages 118 and 119

Introduction

As deliveries go, it was hardly the most taxing I shall ever receive in my cricket career, but it was the most significant one. It was a juicy half-volley on my leg stump, and I gratefully stroked it away through mid-wicket. As I ran to the bowler's end I noticed that the ball was rolling away slowly into the outfield with no fielder anywhere near it. 'Crikey, there's two there,' I thought, and I quickened up my pace between the wickets and safely negotiated the second run. As I reached sanctuary I punched the air gleefully and generally looked fairly pleased with myself. I had just completed the hundredth run on a hot, steamy day in Perth, to reach my first Test century. Greg Matthews, the bowler, shook my hand and grinned, 'You owe me a drink for that ball,' and I was deluged with congratulations from the Australian players and my batting partner Bill Athey. To my delight I managed to pick out my parents in one of the stands; they were on their feet, waving and applauding. Back home in Nottinghamshire my wife Carole was coping with more mundane matters: changing the nappies of our four-month-old son Stuart. She missed the actual stroke that brought up the hundred on the radio (Stuart can be very insistent!), but I knew she would not need to be glued to the commentary to feel as fulfilled and proud as her husband.

That moment from the Australian tour remains my outstanding memory so far in my career. That night I could not sleep, as a whirlpool of emotions crowded in on me: the sheer excitement of doing well for England, the deep satisfaction of proving myself at international level after tasting the big match atmosphere for a tantalizingly short period in the summer of 1984. I felt vindicated for my extreme disappointment when I was passed over by the selectors for England tours in the previous two winters. Within me I had felt capable of performing well at the highest level, yet I had been thwarted and frustrated at every turn since 1984. I had watched my opening partner, Tim Robinson, adapt splendidly to Test cricket while I languished, wondering if Nottinghamshire would ever provide England's opening pair. It had looked more and more unlikely but I never gave up hope. Without that inner core of driving ambition, I would never have made the grade: I knew that self-discipline, concentration and pride in my performance had to compensate for a lack of natural talent that someone like David Gower possesses in such abundance. Now, at the age of twenty-nine, I had achieved something tangible in my career: whatever else happened to me, I had scored a hundred for my country against Australia.

I thought of the lads down at Long Ashton Cricket Club, where I played so many enjoyable matches before I joined the Gloucestershire staff. I hoped they would be raising a glass or two in my direction that night, and I looked forward to endless leg-pulling when I popped in to see them all a few months later. I thought of Reg Sinfield, a former England player himself, and a massive influence on my cricketing philosophy from the days when he had coached me at Colston's School in Bristol. The memory of lying in a hospital bed for two months came flooding back; I did not know it at the time, but my parents had been told that their fifteen-year-old son might not survive an inflammation of the bone marrow and that, at best, he would not be able to resume his love affair with all sports. Above all, I thought of Carole. She was the one who staunchly supported me after I had come to the painful decision to leave Gloucestershire and seek more rewarding employment elsewhere. It was Carole who encouraged me to do myself justice, to move to Nottingham-shire and surmount the inevitable flak that came my way from ill-founded press reports. Without her positive attitude I might just have drifted out of the game. I have always been a fairly fatalistic character – 'Whatever will be, will be' should be my motto – and her support has been vital. I wished she had been there to share my pride that night in Perth, but the needs of our two children came first.

So much has happened in just a few short months. I have been catapulted from the genial camaraderie of the county cricket circuit to the world of agents, chat shows, car phones and acceptance speeches at award ceremonies. I have been telephoned by the likes of Elton John and Phil Collins, inter-viewed by media giants like Terry Wogan and David Frost, and have visited the Sydney home of the great Harold Larwood. All this because I happened to play very well against a fairly moderate Australian bowling line-up over a period of three months. An Alfa Romeo car came my way as a reward for being named International Cricketer of the Year in Australia, ahead of such immortals as Ian Botham, Viv Richards, David Gower and Allan Border. All this is the stuff of schoolboy fiction, but I for one can see it all in perspective. It is all very exciting – and I have always been the type who needs the adrenalin to pump – but I know that it is a shallow world, that the glitter of being a top cricketer can soon fade if the hard grind of work is not being done. The vicissitudes of my career have given me the mental strength to prepare for further reverses, and if the glamour stuff ended tomorrow I would be completely philosophical about it. It is now up to me to maintain my cricketing standards, and everything else will then take care of itself. It is time to take stock of my life and reaffirm my order of priorities. They really are little different from those of the ordinary guy: job satisfaction and family stability. Achieving those two goals has been an interesting experience.

1

A Sickly Youth!

I have lost count of the times I have been described in the press as 'the tall, strapping Broad', with the obligatory analogies to my guardsman's stature. Well I was always tall for my age, and when I started to play good quality rugby at around the age of sixteen a course of weight-training transformed my rather spindly, gangling physique. Yet a year earlier I had faced a sterner struggle than finding some muscle power to survive in the scrum: I faced a battle for life itself.

I was fifteen, mad about sport, a lazy pupil at Colston's School with an easy-going attitude to life that has hardly changed. I was standing at a bus stop after playing rugby at school and wondering why my left hip hurt so much. Some knock picked up in the game, probably – it would clear up after a good night's sleep. The flu symptoms that were dogging me hardly improved my morale, but I would be fit for the next match. Two days later I was delirious and had to be wheeled into an ambulance. My parents were told I had contracted osteomyelitis, an inflammation of the bone marrow. Somehow I had picked up an infection in my left hip which stemmed from the knock in that rugby game. The marrow was septic and an immediate operation was vital. If I was lucky, my left leg would be shortened when the infected marrow was taken out; it would mean a permanent limp and no active sport. If I was unlucky, I would die.

Of course I knew nothing of all this, but my parents were shattered. The gloomy prognosis was kept from me until I was back home recuperating. For the next two months I was on antibiotics, fighting to shake off something I felt was little more than a minor irritation. I had no less than fifty-two injections (twenty-six in each buttock: I felt like a pin cushion!), and I was put on traction. I was strapped all the way down my left leg, with weights keeping it extended to avoid ending up with one leg shorter than the other. The muscle loss was incredible, but I could live with that. Playing sport was more important; I had no idea that the surgeons had performed a miracle in saving my life *and* maintaining the length of my leg. There were some consolations during my stay in hospital. It was a great Christmas – the nurses really spoiled me! – and I had a request read out on Ed Stewart's radio programme on the BBC. Alan Morley, the England rugby winger and an old boy from my school, sent me a programme of the Wales match, signed by all the players, as well as a signed photograph of Alan scoring a try against South Africa.

When I left hospital all I wanted to do was play rugby again and get fit for the cricket season. No such luck – I had to walk on crutches for a time, and I lost almost a year to osteomyelitis. It could have been worse. Now, with two children of my own, I can imagine what hell my parents went through during the last few weeks of 1972. All I could offer was the impatience of youth, the frustration of spending the rugby season on my back, moaning about those boring exercises with the weights.

It was not as if I was a stranger to hospitals. I seemed to

spend a lot of time talking to nurses in my youth: a broken arm, a split finger, a chipped bone in a thumb, a broken nose, a cartilage operation and the removal of my appendix, which left me with an enormous, ugly scar. Hopefully I have got all the serious injuries and illnesses out of the way in my adolescence, although a family tragedy in 1982 made me realize how fallible we all are. My brother Mike died of a massive heart attack at the age of twenty-six. A keen rugby player, tall and slim, you would never believe he was a candidate for something like that. He had been very depressed before taking a holiday in Spain, but he returned tanned and relaxed and we all felt relieved for him. My father found him slumped against the bedroom door after he had failed to report to work. It was a terrible shock, and for a couple of years after that I feared the worst every time I had the slightest pain in my chest. Did heart disease run in the family, I wondered? Finally I realized I was becoming a hypochondriac about chest pains, and I had a medical, which banished my fears, but something like Mike's death puts all our minor problems into sharper focus.

So we were unlucky with that tragic loss, but in all other respects our family enjoyed a very comfortable existence in Bristol. My father had his own building business, passed down from his father, and we never really lacked for anything. Dad always played good club cricket in the area, and I remember regular visits to Stoke Bishop Cricket Club and fish and chip suppers on the way home after the game. It seemed a very pleasant way to pass the time and soon I was getting on the pitch. One day I picked up a bat with my left hand and batted that way. There was no significance to it: I am right-handed in everything else.

From prep school I went to Colston's School and quickly settled into the sporting atmosphere. Rugby in the winter, cricket in the summer, as well as any other sports that were available. I eventually played rugby for England Colleges, Bristol United, and then Clifton, and I particularly enjoyed the fitness training. I was shrewd enough to avoid much of the roughhouse stuff among the forwards – I always seemed to be more interested in the next phase of play! – but that also summed up my lazy attitude to life in general. It was hardly a great struggle for me to excel in sport at school and I just took it for granted, doing no extra training. At fifteen I was in the first eleven at cricket and the first fifteen at rugby, but I took it all very light-heartedly. I would go along to the county ground at Bristol, start to watch the cricket, get bored, and my father would eventually find me playing round the back with a bat and ball and some new-found friends. Failing that, I would be in the queue for autographs, just like all the rest. I had no idea why; it just seemed a good idea at the time. Dennis Amiss was one of my prized captures, and I valued any other Test player – I was fairly choosy! One of the players to sign for me was Bob Willis: a decade later he would be alongside me for my Test debut, and even later he would be in the Channel Nine commentary box, passing expert comments on my three centuries in the Ashes Series.

Even at the age of fifteen I had no desire to play alongside adults in club cricket. I was perfectly happy with the standard in schools games and had no real inclination to improve myself. Reg Sinfield was the man who did most during that period to clear away my woolly thinking, my lackadaisical approach to sport and life. Reg was in charge of all our sporting gear at school and he would also umpire our games. A great conversationalist, he loved to tell us about bowling to Don Bradman, how great a player Wally Hammond was, and all the tales from his Gloucestershire days. They were just names to us, but Reg was such a genial, kind man that we were never bored. He had, after all, played for England and no one could ever take that away from him. His knowledge was vast: I would always want to stand beside him at square leg during matches and find out about the state of the wicket from him. He has always been a stickler for fair play and I like to think I picked up similar principles from Reg. I could talk to him about any problems, sporting or otherwise, and among cricketers he remains the biggest influence on me. Even now I go to see him when I can at Colston's School, and he is always there, stitching a pad or mending a hockey bat, ready to chat or listen. It was typical of Reg that he should write to Peter May, chairman of the England selectors, as long ago as 1983 to recommend that he should take a look at me. I have no idea if Peter May followed Reg's advice but, although such a recommendation was rather premature at that stage in my career, I was touched by the gesture.

Above all, Reg Sinfield passed on his love of cricket to me. I remember how proud he was to present a brand new Gray–Nicholls bat to me at morning assembly after I had scored a hundred for the school against Prior Park College. That bat lasted me two full seasons and it seemed to inspire me to a string of high scores. I had finally conquered my lethargy and decided to play adult cricket, first with the Downend Club (where W. G. Grace learned to play more than a century earlier), then with Long Ashton. In my first Sunday game for them I made 96, and the following week 99: it really was a very good bat! I had my first experience of touring with Long Ashton and I loved the pranks and the high spirits. Long Ashton Cricket Club will always hold a special place in my affections because they were a successful side who played good quality cricket, but they also enjoyed themselves. As a shy, angular lad, I needed to be brought more out of myself, and they were terrific to me. People like Les Hodge, Paul Trineman and John Sullivan encouraged me all the time and gave me the chance to improve. John Sullivan was the first opening partner that I really respected. He had played for Gloucestershire and he was simply too good for our local league; he regularly averaged seventy a season and he taught me a great deal. I changed beside him in the dressing-room, asked him to explain aspects of the game to me and it was a thrill to open the batting with him. Even now, when I go back to see the lads at Long Ashton, I have a great respect for John Sullivan and I recall with great pride the day that I actually outscored him in a century stand. Long Ashton CC is one of the places where I can always relax, where people do not expect me to be anything other than a normal chap. A hearty smack on the back, an invitation to step up to the bar, and a happy group of down-to-earth characters all add up to a very important place for me, and so it will remain.

If my cricket was developing, my academic career was sadly not keeping pace. I picked up five O Levels, enough to get me into St Paul's College in Cheltenham to train as a teacher, but I was never going to be an academic high-flyer. A lazy mind and serene disposition did not equip me for the stern examinations in lecture rooms, and after a year I switched to a course in recreational management. The idea was to learn how to run sports centres and that appealed to me more than standing up in a class full of children. I only lasted a year on that course, however: suddenly a career in cricket beckoned.

My success with Long Ashton had brought me a few games with Gloucestershire's Club and Ground team, then the Second Eleven. Before that, I was playing for Gloucestershire Under-19s and Gloucestershire Young Cricketers. At the age of nineteen I played at Lord's for the first time, for the National Association of Young Cricketers against MCC Schools. Four England players of the future appeared in that game – Derek Pringle, Paul Terry, Jonathan Agnew and myself – as well as Robin Dyer and Mike Garnham, and it was a tremendous experience to play at Lord's, even if the ground was empty. In that summer of 1977 I also played with a certain Allan Border for Gloucestershire Seconds and against Tim Boon, Geoff Marsh and Tim Zoehrer who were over here with the Australian Schools team. I regret to say that none of them made any impression on me; a decade later we would be locked in sterner combat.

During this period I had a vague idea that it would be nice to play cricket for a living, but I had no idea if I would be good enough. I had a variety of jobs: a hotel porter, a carpet fitter, and packing lorries in a warehouse at night while listening to the radio commentaries of England beating Australia 5–1 under Mike Brearley. Gloucestershire took me on a short tour of Malawi in the autumn of 1978 and I must have impressed them because they offered me a one-year contract for the 1979 season. It was worth £2,000 but I cared little for the money at that stage, even though I had met Carole at college and we had decided to get married. Suddenly all the other available professional doors had closed. I realized that I lacked the mental clarity to prosper in recreational management or the extrovert personality to be a teacher. Options were severely limited and I was curious to know just how good I could be at professional cricket.

It amuses me now to read newspaper profiles describing my alleged single-mindedness about my cricket career. It is true that I have buckled down to the mental demands, that I now try very hard to make everything count, that I am very ambitious for myself and whichever team I represent – but that was not always the case. I was no Boycott, spurning all the other pleasures of life in favour of an obsessive determination to triumph over insuperable odds. I just drifted into a professional cricket career after letting the world go by for a long time. I have been a late developer in most facets of my life: I was still collecting autographs at fifteen, when one should have grown out of that a few years earlier, and I must have been at least seventeen before I ever shaved. I came late to adult cricket and I was twenty-one before I played for Gloucestershire. Basically I just coasted along until 1979, content that something of interest would turn up. Professional cricket was that something and it was time to knuckle down to a job for once in my life.

2

Early Years as a County Professional

The year 1979 was a momentous one for me. I got married, and in my twenty-second year I finally landed a proper job. It was to do something that every cricket fan dreams about: to play the game for a living. The fact that I was being paid to represent my home county meant a great deal to me and, despite all the subsequent disagreements and frustration, I shall always be grateful to Gloucestershire for giving me the chance to get stuck in and make something of myself instead of drifting along aimlessly. Carole was also invaluable in that direction. We had met at college where she qualified in graphic art; she ending up teaching for four years until our daughter Gemma was born. So Carole was making something of herself professionally and she expected me to do the same.

I was lucky to attract the attention of Gloucestershire at a time when the club was going through a period of transition. They had won the Benson and Hedges Cup in 1977 and only narrowly missed out on the Championship that season. But that was the peak year: Mike Procter could work miracles for only so many years and the other two overseas players – Zaheer Abbas and Sadiq Mohammad – were sporadic match-winners. We were short of penetrative bowlers, with the veterans Brian Brain and Procter our only class performers. The batting was far from settled at the start of the 1979 season, and there was plenty of scope for any young ambitious player. I had been on the fringe of things for a couple of seasons, playing alongside David Graveney, Jim Foat and Andy Stovold for the Under-25s, and I was a keen supporter. When we won the Benson and Hedges Cup I went to Lord's as a fan to cheer the boys on. In fact the County Year Book which featured a photo that year of Mike Procter brandishing the trophy also captured me in the background, lapping up the atmosphere. I had steeled myself to run on to the pitch at the end of the game and it was a great feeling to relish my home county's glory. Even then, within sight of my twentieth birthday, I had no ambitions to play for Gloucestershire: it was simply an enjoyable day out to watch some acquaintances of mine play very well. Two years later I would be sharing a dressing-room with these household names.

Mike Procter was the most outstanding cricketer for Gloucestershire since Wally Hammond, and his inspirational qualities had galvanized the side for a decade. I never really got to know him in the three seasons I played under his captaincy. He was not a great communicator, preferring to lead by example in the manner of his fellow South African Clive Rice, who later captained me at Trent Bridge. Procter's knees were troubling him by 1979 and his great days with the ball were becoming less frequent, but he was still a master batsman. He may have been troubled by high pace but he would murder the medium-pacers and spinners. He would walk inside the line and hit the spinners over extra cover time and again. Many people in the Gloucestershire and Somerset area at that time used to try to compare the batting abilities of Procter and Botham, the two great all-rounders, and I always thought that Procter was a better batsman than Ian

Botham. To me, a spinner has always been a good bet against Botham because he seems to premeditate his shot on occasions, and cannot alter the stroke if the ball turns or holds up. On the other hand Procter was always so controlled against spin, so certain in his strokeplay. When he put his mind to the job he was devastating and his sound technique stood him in good stead when the ball was turning. Every summer he would set himself to score the fastest hundred of the season, and invariably he would get there towards the end of the summer. I suppose he needed to be fired up in search of such goals because he knew that Gloucestershire would not be winning any trophies and he would not be playing Test cricket. Whatever his motivation, Mike Procter was a great sight when he got after the bowlers.

For all his all-round brilliance, I never learned all that much from Procter. He did teach me one thing, though, and it impressed me at the time. Within a month of my making the First team, he told me to bowl in a John Player League game against Somerset. I told him I was not a good bowler, but he insisted. An analysis of 0 for 18 in 4 overs is hardly impressive, but the captain was right to insist. He said that everyone who played first-class cricket should be able to turn his hand to all facets of the game if necessary, because that helped a player in his specific discipline. Regrettably that was a rare example that I saw of Procter's approach to the game; I never really saw him open up in front of the team and talk through important issues. Some of my team-mates would tell me he was a great socializer, but he would need a few drinks to loosen up – and then he would be fascinating on the game. I never saw that side of him because I was not always in the First team and therefore comparatively insignificant. I still had so much to learn about the hard, professional nature of cricket, a point graphically underlined in a Championship match against Somerset towards the end of my first season.

We should have won the game after a run chase, but I stagnated, could not get the ball away and failed to give enough of the strike to Zaheer Abbas. Zed did not seem to mind – he was always very keen on personal milestones and on this day he got another century – but I understand that Procter was fuming about us as he watched from the dressing-room. I was too inexperienced to grasp the tactical nuances: all I could think was, 'Zed will get these, he doesn't need much help from me,' but I was sadly wrong. I should have tried harder to give Zed the strike, run the singles very quickly and forgotten about my inability to get the ball away for boundaries. After failing to do that, I should have been taken to one side and told in no uncertain terms by the captain where I had gone wrong. Procter did not say a word to me: I had to hear about his annoyance from friends in the side.

I first met Zaheer when he was playing for the Club and Ground. We piled into his old yellow Volkswagen and turned up at an RAF camp to play a warm-up match at the start of a season. When we batted together, all he said to me was, 'You must run your first single very, very quick – very, very quick.' I later realized the significance of the remark: Zed was a great counter when he wanted the strike. He loved to reach personal goals and it meant a great deal to him to become the first Asian to reach a hundred centuries. Zed had a remarkable eye and a fantastic pair of wrists with which he could manipulate the ball in all sorts of directions. He did not like genuine fast bowling, yet he could still score off it in his own way. I once batted with him at the Oval, when Sylvester Clarke was roaring in with one or two points to prove: Clarke had got into trouble in Pakistan for throwing a brick into the crowd during a Test match and he was not over-enamoured with Pakistanis. He really gave Zed a going-over, but Zed struck him all over the place, stepping back towards square leg to hit the ball through the covers, chipping him through gully and moving across his stumps to whack him over mid-wicket. I am sure that Zed was worried about being hit but it was still an amazing piece of batting.

Zed had a very low pain threshold. I once collided with him in the middle of the pitch as we went for a second run and I shall never forget the sight of him spiralling in the air, then collapsing in a heap in his crease. Now I know that I was built on rather more powerful lines than the sleek Pakistani, but the collision was a fairly light one and I hardly felt any impact. Yet Zed retired hurt, looking thoroughly miserable, and did not play in the next game. He often worried about colds and high temperatures, and we always knew that he was not a hundred-per-cent team man – few great batsmen are – but he was a marvellous sight when in full flow and I count myself lucky to have watched his wizardry from the other end of the wicket.

The other Pakistani on our books in my first season on the staff was a different character. I really liked Sadiq Mohammad. When he was dropped to make way for me in a Benson and Hedges match, he was kindness itself; other players of his stature would have sulked, but he went out of his way to help a young player. A very hard worker in the nets and a jaunty, funny character, Sadiq was good value and deservedly popular. As a fellow left-hander he seemed to want to help me and his attitude was an interesting contrast to his more illustrious overseas colleagues in our team.

I could not really complain, though. I loved the challenge of my first season, the thrill of playing with and against great players. I tried to watch every ball when I was not out in the middle, wondering what the bowlers were trying to do and how the batsmen were combating them. I may have arrived comparatively late on the county scene, but I was hungry for knowledge. When I made my first-class début, I almost marked the occasion with a hundred, but had to settle for 86.

Steve Windaybank, also making his first-class début, opened with me and we put on over a hundred. The wicket was flawless, the bowling friendly and as I got nearer to the century mark, my team-mates kept telling me I could emulate the achievement of David Shepherd, the only player in the county's history to make a hundred on his first-class début. That preyed on my mind and I spooned a catch to mid-on as I tried to play the ball through mid-wicket. Disappointing, of course, but not a bad way to start a first-class career. The county coach, Graham Wiltshire, clearly thought so because next day I received a telegram at the ground: *Well done. Now you've set the standard keep it going. Coach and boss.* A few days later I was opening another telegram at Swansea: *Good luck Broadstairs. Long Ashton C.C.* – this to mark my first game in the Benson and Hedges Cup when Sadiq was dropped to make way for me.

I have vivid memories of that first summer in county cricket, even if I did not play all that many games. I caught Viv Richards first ball at Taunton after Brian Brain had told everyone he was going to try to bounce him out. We all laughed at him – 'Great idea, Brainy, Viv should love that!' – but it worked. Viv top-edged the hook shot and I caught him down at fine leg. When the ball was safely in my hands I looked up and saw Brainy just ten yards away from me. He had run all the way from his end to ensure he would get the rebound if I dropped it. Not a bad compliment to the great West Indian from a bowler old enough to have bowled at Peter May! My first hundred in first-class cricket came in the last game of the season, after a near-miss the previous match against Warwickshire. I had got to 96 when Steve Perryman bowled what I thought was a juicy half-volley. I leaned into it and smacked it straight to Dennis Amiss at extra cover. There was much wailing and gnashing of teeth in the Broad household, but I managed to get there a few days later. I can still see the dreadful shot I played to reach three figures: Peter Willey bowled one that went on with his arm and I got an inside edge to squirt it away for a couple of runs. That night he congratulated me in the bar and I said that I had spoiled it a little by playing such an awful shot off his bowling. 'Don't worry how you get 'em, just get 'em,' he replied. I thought that a tremendous comment from an England player to a young hopeful who could easily fade from the scene. Because of encouragement from senior respected players like Peter Willey, I have tried to follow such an example as I progressed in the game. I value such good fellowship on the county circuit very highly.

An average of 36 from 500 first-class runs was a satisfactory return from my début season, I felt. The club eased me gently into the serious stuff, and I loved it. Some are mentally exhausted after stepping up from Second Eleven cricket to the First team, but I found it all very exhilarating. The social side was terrific: Gloucestershire invariably seem to get that right. A guy like David Shepherd was a tonic to be with because he gave great entertainment on the field and amused everyone in the bar or in the dressing-room. Andy Brassington's infectious enthusiasm and cheeky charm always brought a laugh and we used to love it when Brian Brain had a good old moan. On a professional level, Graham Wiltshire's note after my hundred against Northants left a deep impression: *Wonderful. Well done. Now for 150.* I was well aware that consistent large scores were needed. The second season would find out my true worth.

Before my second season on the full-time staff I spent an unhappy time in Australia. The sequence of events led to my first niggle with Gloucestershire and it still rankles with me that they did not support me fully in my dispute. Shaun Graf had played a few Second Eleven games with me, then moved to Hampshire but kept in touch. One day he rang me up and asked if I would be interested in going out to Melbourne to play for Somerville, a club coached by his brother. It seemed an ideal opportunity to develop my technique and to take coaching clinics, but it was not a success. We played on tar-based pitches so that when the sun came out they became sticky and dangerous. I did not care for all the 'sledging', the foul-mouthed abuse that had been popularized by the Australian Test side. England were over there that summer and as we proceeded to lose the series by 3–0, the anti-Pommie crowing became a pain in the neck. The quality of cricket was poor, and I missed the good fellowship and manners of the English version. Things came to a head when Carole and I decided to take a holiday on the Great Barrier Reef at the same time as Somerville had reached the semi-finals of a cup competition. The club was furious that I was unavailable, but I had tried for some time to find out the date of the match and they were simply too slapdash about getting the information. We parted on bad terms and the Victorian Cricket Association wrote to Gloucestershire's Secretary, Tony Brown, to say that I would be banned from all cricket in the state of Victoria unless I apologized. I felt very embarrassed when Tony Brown showed me the letter, and angry that my side of the saga had not been fully appreciated. I was asked to write a letter of apology, even though Shaun Graf's promise of car, job and accommodation had not materialized. The reality was that I had no job for seven weeks, we had to lodge with an old lady who did not want us in the house, and we shared a broken-down Volkswagen of 1969 vintage. I believe Shaun Graf organized the letter to Gloucestershire because I cannot imagine that the influential officials of the Victorian Cricket Association would be the slightest bit interested in a dispute of such insignificance. The fact that the VCA sent me a very warm, effusive telegram of congratulations on my England début four years later makes me even more suspicious. I have often wondered if some people at the club believed I was beginning to establish a reputation for being 'difficult' – an allegation which gained extra credence in the troubled summer of 1983. To me it was simply a case of sticking up for my rights and fighting on a principle.

By the time the 1980 season started I had put the Somerville episode behind me, although it surfaced again when we played Hampshire at Cheltenham. I scored a hundred against Shaun Graf's bowling and ran him out, to my unconcealed glee. More relevantly I moved up to a regular opening berth in the First team and learned a lot. I fell just short of 1,000 first-class runs, but was dropped for a time. It was a correct decision, although it bothered me at the time. The problem was that I was getting 20s and 30s but not progressing to big scores. It seemed a shame that I had to approach Mike Procter to ask why I had been dropped, rather than a young player getting a quiet word in his ear, but at least he spoke some home truths when I raised the subject. The truth was I was still a long way short of an acceptable standard, even if I did manage to get three first-class hundreds that summer. One of them was against the undemanding bowlers of Oxford University, when I posted a hundred before lunch as early as 23 April. That unexceptional feat even made me the subject of a Roy Ulyett cartoon in the *Daily Express* the following day – it must have been a slack news day in the sporting world. Another hundred against Warwickshire brought me my first Man-of-the-Match award and a kind word of encouragement from a player who was to become a good friend, Andy Lloyd. Now Andy was just starting out on his county career as well – that is why he was standing at short leg to the bowling of Dilip Doshi! – and he was aghast as I tried to sweep the left-arm spinner when I was in the 90s. 'For ... sake, don't start sweeping at this stage!' said Andy. 'Get your head down and play properly!' Old-fashioned advice from a callow lad of twenty-three, but it was good advice.

My experience against the wiles of Dilip Doshi underlined that I had little confidence against the spinners. On the flat low pitches at Bristol I would simply push forward against all bowlers and accumulate. Because I lacked confidence against the turning ball I would try to hit the spinner in the air, not realizing that it was not a shot for a percentage player like me. I do not like lofting the ball because I lack the power and timing of a Procter or a Botham. I still rely a great deal on the ball coming on to the bat and being able to deflect it away through the gaps. The suggestion that I did not fancy spin bowling was soon bandied around when I came into county cricket and they were right. I would either lose patience ('I'll show them who can play this stuff!') or someone like Derek Underwood would turn me inside out with his guile and variation. Good judges say that Underwood never likes bowling at left-handers but I was never aware of that! I needed hours of practice against spin in the nets, but although John Childs and David Graveney spent time with me in the nets, I still lacked total conviction against spin in general. So I was stuck with the tag of being a poor player of the spinners, and it is still with me today to a certain extent.

Throughout the 1981 summer I was worried about being dropped. I started the season poorly so I borrowed Zaheer's helmet and used a new bat, and it seemed to work for a time as my form picked up. Insecurity was still nagging away at me and I know my good friend Phil Bainbridge felt the same. We had struck up a firm friendship that has lasted to this day and we had much in common: we were both involved in teacher training, both joined the full-time staff in the same year, we were married in the same year, had children within a week of each other and were even capped on the same day. Phil and I were amazed that we were given our county caps so early; we were both on our way to a thousand runs for the first time in our careers in 1981, but we always felt we were unsure of our places in the side. I can recall regular occasions when our wives would turn up on the first morning of a match and ask anxiously, 'Are you playing?' Perhaps the club sensed our insecurity and they capped us as a gesture of confidence; whatever their motives, we did not really deserve the honour. I was still learning the game, not sure if I would be able to come out a better player from a bad spell. The county circuit really suited me and I was making friendships that will last a long time, but I knew that I had to start developing my technique and acquiring the concentration to build big scores. To me an average of around 30 was not good enough, it was mediocre. The good players averaged over 40 and the rest were just a supporting cast.

Within a year we were to lose three of our most talented players – Procter, Brain and Sadiq – while Zaheer's appearances started to dwindle, due to Test and World Cup calls and a declining appetite for the county game. The old order was changing and things did not look very bright. The retirement of Brain and Procter left the bowling department threadbare; we had relied on them for far too long anyway, and not even Procter's guts and Brain's lovely action could withstand the ravages of time. The batsmen knew that the stick we would receive from opposition fast bowlers would not now be answered from our side. The face of Gloucestershire cricket was soon to be radically altered. The same applied to my life and cricket career.

3

The Road from Bristol

Ironically it was my best friend in the game who unwittingly planted the seed that flowered into the discontent which forced me to leave Bristol. Phil Bainbridge and I were having one of our usual heart-to-hearts over a beer in the bar at the Nevil Road ground when he started to indulge in a bit of a moan. It was the usual stuff we all offer when the side is playing poorly or – even more relevantly – when you are going through a bad trot. Phil even uttered the apparent heresy that it would be better to leave the county and try to prosper in the game somewhere else. At the time, I was surprised. 'How can you say that?' I said, 'We're enjoying ourselves, aren't we?' In a social sense that was true. Generally all the players got on very well and specifically the Broads, Bainbridges and Hignells were very close – we are all god-parents to our respective children, after all. Yet Bains had touched on a sensitive issue and I mulled it over for some time afterwards. The team was going through a transitional stage after the departure of Procter and the prospects were far from rosy. The stars were leaving the stage, the Bristol public had given up on us in favour of the more glamorous action down in Taunton, and the solid journeymen in the First team could not fill the gaps. I was far from happy with my own progress: an opener cannot learn all that much about his trade if he knows he just has to push forward on the slow low Bristol wicket and graft his way to a boring 40-odd. The priority for me was to enjoy my cricket with a team that was doing well on the field. An average of 28 for B. C. Broad and just two Championship wins in the 1982 season hardly indicated that those two targets were being handsomely attained.

I brooded about my future throughout the winter of 1982. There were consolations, not least of all a marvellous period in New Zealand. I managed to land a playing and coaching contract with Takapuna CC near Auckland. The captaincy of the side was an extra incentive to do well and Carole and I loved the life out there. It was such a pleasant contrast to the unhappy period spent in Melbourne three years earlier and the good manners on the field compared very favourably with the boorishness of some of the Australians. I was very grateful to Graeme Fowler for recommending me to Takapuna – he had to turn down the offer due to more pressing engagements with England! – and I was pleased that my foresight in attaining an advanced coaching certificate in 1981 had paid off. I am sure that my coaching qualification landed me the job, because there would have been many other English professionals in contention as well as a young batsman from a struggling county who was still trying to establish himself in the English county circuit.

Would I finally manage that in the summer of 1983? Was I at fault, or was the organization of the club one of the major factors? It was so hard to separate the little niggles from the vital issues. Take the day that Phil Bainbridge and I were awarded our county caps in 1981: in fact that is one thing we did not actually receive. All we got was a handshake from

Mike Procter in the dressing-room and a promise that we would be able to wear our caps in due course. Apparently the club had no caps available and they had to send off to Pakistan for them. It may sound trivial but we were upset about that: we were very proud of the award, even though we felt we were lucky to get it so soon in our respective careers. When I walked out to bat and the public address announced I had been capped, I had to smile. Would I mind waiting a while before I could actually put it on my head? It was so sloppy and, to a Gloucestershire man like me, an anti-climax. Any professional sportsman likes to achieve personal targets and that was one of my most important achievements so far. I wanted tangible recognition of that.

Clearly there were problems at Gloucestershire CCC. The club was losing around a thousand pounds a week at that time and it was difficult to concentrate on the job out there on the pitch when we were unsure if we would still have employment in the near future. There was hardly any public support and we did not really deserve any. Tony Brown left in the winter of 1982 to join Somerset. I think he was right to go: he had been with the club as player, captain and secretary for more than a quarter of a century and perhaps – as I was to discover two years later – a change of scenery was beneficial. It would be some time before the players and captain could do themselves justice in a more stable atmosphere at Bristol and I was not sure I could wait around that long, stagnating and unfulfilled.

One or two newspaper articles about my England credentials did not ease my restlessness. In the winter of 1982–3 England still had problems with their openers. With Graham Gooch and many others banned for their South African connections, there was a vacancy or two at the top of the order, and Geoff Cook, Chris Tavaré and Graeme Fowler had not really impressed on the tour of Australasia. My parents sent me out a press cutting to New Zealand in which Scyld Berry of the *Observer* discussed options among the openers: Alan Butcher of Surrey got a mention, so did Wilf Slack of Middlesex and, to my surprise so did I. Just four seasons in the county game, a handful of first-class centuries and here I was, getting a favourable mention! Now it is true that I had got a marvellous press for an innings of 98 against Middlesex in the quarter-finals of the NatWest Bank Trophy in the previous summer and although I considered it my best performance to date, it hardly seemed the most impressive of credentials. I was still a limited player, operating in a poor team, and still very much the young apprentice. Yet why should I not dream my dreams? I needed goals to keep me going, and one of them was an England place. It seemed to me that an unattainable target was preferable to just jogging along, because if you fell short of the highest prize you would at least have improved as a player. Perhaps I became too obvious in my ambitions after the winter of 1982–3: I know some thought I was now a bit of a 'show pony', going on about playing for England after being in the senior game for about five minutes. To me it was simply a case of being honest; when asked the question I would always add the rider that I still had much to do to be worthy of such an honour, but that I would do everything in my power to get there. I did not add that it might involve moving to another county.

My England credentials were even discussed at Gloucestershire's AGM that winter. Don Perry, the club Chairman, stood up and said, 'When Chris looks at the performance of the England players in Australia, he must be kicking himself for the chance he allowed to pass by.' I could not really see how I had 'allowed' myself to be passed over. Perry warmed to his theme: 'Chris could have established himself as a leading member of the tour party and it is up to him to become an England cricketer if he has the will.' I did not agree with the first part of that statement – I was neither good nor experienced enough in 1982 – but the idea of enforcing my will to improve my career was not lost on me.

Don Perry was not the only influential man at Bristol to feel I was an England prospect. David Graveney, the captain and Acting Secretary, wrote to me in New Zealand and produced some telling words: 'No doubt the exploits in Australia or the lack of them have not gone unnoticed and I feel that 1983 is the perfect time for you to push for an international place. Therefore it is important to put together performances right from the start.' David went on to say that he had no doubts at all about my ability, even though the previous season had been so disappointing. Then came the most telling thrust:

> 'Your worst enemy is yourself. I remember very well having a discussion with you at Hove a few years ago, where we discussed at great length your approach to the game. If you think that I am the only person who thinks this way, this suggestion was further underlined by an England selector, who informed me that though they had a high regard for your ability, particularly against quick bowling, they still had reservations regarding your attitude.'

I never found out who that selector was, but a month later I discovered that a high-ranking England official did not know me from a New Zealand opening bowler. I was at a party for the England players in Auckland given by Clive Radley, and the official was in attendance. I am indebted to my wife Carole for the revelation that he asked who the tall chap was and did he bat or bowl. Carole has always been a high-class eavesdropper!

So it was all very well for David Graveney and Don Perry to go on about my credentials for representing my country but I was at no stage taking such a prospect seriously, apart from telling myself I must improve my batting. I have no real idea what David meant by my 'attitude' – perhaps echoes of the Shaun Graf incident in Melbourne a few years earlier? Perhaps I had been sulking rather too much, a tendency that used to surface whenever I was out cheaply or to a bad shot. I always had a bit of a rebellious streak in me and a rather immature way of expressing my views, but as my career became established at Bristol I genuinely felt my observations had been fairly and honestly expressed, face-to-face.

At the start of the 1983 season I had no intentions of moping around, yet I got sucked into the general malaise around the county ground. I was absolutely determined to become a more consistent batsman and that if I was not enjoying my cricket I should either change counties or give up the game. Nagging away at the back of my mind was the fact that my three-year contract was due to expire in September: that would represent an ideal opportunity to leave without any undue acrimony or at least to sort myself out and commit myself to Bristol for the rest of my career. Either way I had some hard thinking ahead of me in the next couple of months. The experience was to prove a traumatic one.

4

The Road to Trent Bridge

If Phil Bainbridge had sown the seed of disillusionment a season earlier, it was Andy Stovold who helped the plant bloom. Not that Andy was aware of that – he was too busy reeling off centuries in May 1983. I was opening with Andy that season and he played magnificently that month. His timing was superb, his strokeplay varied and audacious, and I could not believe there was a better opening batsman available to England at that stage. With the World Cup due to be staged a month later, Andy Stovold seemed the ideal opener for the occasion. Yet Graeme Fowler and Chris Tavaré again got the vote. It seemed so unfair on Andy, and I began to think that no one from Gloucestershire would ever play for England unless we were top of the Championship table. I hasten to add that I did not include myself in the category of England possibles that season; it was simply that if I ever attained consistency and a tight enough technique, it would be nice to feel the England selectors would notice me.

As Stovold's partner I was averaging 45 in Championship cricket until Kent's Kevin Jarvis cracked a bone in my right wrist in June. I was out for a month and that gave me enough time to sort out my future. After hours of heart-searching and discussions with Carole, the painful decision was taken. I would tell Gloucestershire that I would be leaving at the end of the season. All the time it had been gnawing away at me that I had to get something better and more enjoyable from my chosen profession. We still had our larks in the dressing-room and laughs on the county circuit, but despite my fondness for most of my team-mates, I simply felt that we were not the players to take Gloucestershire into a new exciting era. I had seen it coming for several years as Procter and Zaheer were allowed to arrive from abroad as late as possible in April, then depart at the season's end. They had not put enough into the club's future, apart from marvellous personal performances, and the vacuum was huge when they left. Players like myself, David Graveney, Andy Stovold, John Childs and Phil Bainbridge were not outstanding enough to stem the tide of mediocrity that engulfed the team. I am sorry to say this about David Graveney because I like and respect him and would always be happy to have a chat with him in the bar, but out there on the pitch he was not assertive enough. It is true he had a poor side, with popguns instead of heavy artillery with the new ball, and he was intelligent enough also to recognize his own limitations as a player, but that was no good to us. We needed either a great player (preferably an all-rounder) to inspire us by his own personal performances, or a wily tactician in the Brearley or Fletcher mould. David Graveney, an unselfish team man, was the only one to do the job in 1983, but even so, it was not going well enough. I must make it clear that I had no designs at all on the captaincy: I still did not know enough about the game and I was more concerned in improving my batting to justify my ambitions. There were simply no other captaincy candidates on the staff. We needed bricks and mortar, not piles of straw dispensed by a civilized, likeable man.

At the end of June I informed the new Secretary, David
Collier, that I would be seeking a move at the end of the
season. The Cricket Committee Chairman, Don Stone, was
called in to see me and immediately got the wrong impression.
He thought it was simply a personality issue between myself
and David Graveney and that some straight talking round a
table between the three of us would sort it all out. I knew
there was no point, because David could not alter the way
he was as captain and individual, nor would I expect him to
do so. I had enough respect for the institution of captaincy
to conclude that it must be the discontented player who leaves
rather than the man in charge. Eventually I got through to
Don Stone who agreed to my release with the proviso that I
would not be offered a contract for 1984 by Gloucestershire
if no other county came in for me. That subtle little bribe
only served to harden my resolve further. I would not be
pressurized: I would leave the game rather than go back on
my decision. I had no idea if any other county would be
interested in me; nobody approached me until late in the
summer when my imminent departure was announced, and
the proper channels of communication were always followed.

Quite simply the side was fatalistic. We did not expect to
win many games; we were going through the motions and
David was not doing enough to take us by the scruff of
the neck and pull the thing around. Two games in August
epitomized that, only serving to underline my conviction that
I was making the correct decision. In the quarter finals of the
NatWest Trophy, Paul Romaines and I put on 95 for the first
wicket, and with Paul continuing to play well we were 149
for 1 with plenty of overs in hand. We needed a massive score
against Hampshire's strong batting, but the innings subsided
gently to 252 for 8 in our 60 overs. I was furious at the way
we had thrown away the advantage, especially after Paul and
I had kept out Malcolm Marshall in the early stages and I

am sorry to say that I took that attitude on to the field when Hampshire batted. I reverted to my old schoolboy sulks and did not concentrate hard enough or field at all keenly. Hampshire won by six wickets with two overs to spare, and I was desperately unhappy at the manner of our defeat and at my immature reaction. Ten days later it happened again, this time at Cheltenham against Yorkshire in a John Player League game. In our 40 overs we made 233 for 5, with 96 from me and an opening stand of 80 between Andy Stovold and myself. We managed to lose by four wickets after an abysmal performance in the field. When the pressure was on, we would bowl and field badly, and these two games were symptomatic of the malaise.

I now wish I had said something to the senior players before the news broke of my release. It just seemed to me at the time that their reaction might be 'Who the hell do you think you are? Why don't you pull your weight in the field and suggest a few things?' so I kept quiet. At least my form picked up once the die had been cast (perhaps my relief showed in my batting) and I scored three centuries in my last four Championship games. It was during that final match, against Nottinghamshire, that all the fuss began about my alleged 'sacking' and all the adverse press comment arose that still rankles with me to this day.

Let me say that if David Collier had been left to organize my departure from the club, it would have been handled in a sensible, civilized manner with none of the rancorous headlines that flew around. I would have been able to see out the rest of the season as well, giving of my best to the club that had offered me a chance just a few years back. I had developed a great respect for David Collier since he took over from Tony Brown and he deserves a lot of credit for transforming Gloucestershire in recent seasons. On Friday 26 August I phoned David to check that our agreed statement to the media about my departure would be issued the following Monday, the second day of our home match against Nottinghamshire. He confirmed that. On the Sunday David told me that the Chairman, Don Perry, had blocked the statement until the Tuesday.

My resentment was still simmering as I walked off the field at Bristol on the Monday night because I had been told to sit on the story for another day. As I left the field, I looked up to the players' balcony and saw Perry locked in discussion with Graham Russell, a freelance journalist based in Bristol and a familiar figure at the ground. In my paranoia I figured that Graham was getting first bite at the story while the central character in the saga had been told to keep his mouth shut for another day. An hour later I happened to be standing in the bar when Graham Russell came up for a chat. It did not need the highest journalistic skills to winkle the story out of me, and Graham duly ran it the following morning in the *Western Daily Press*. 'Broad Drops a Bombshell' screamed the headline, but the story was sensibly and soberly told. I was glad he made the point in the third paragraph that 'Ambition – not money – is driving him away', and I was quoted in only three short paragraphs. The crucial sentences were these: 'Hard though it is, I can't see Gloucestershire getting anywhere. John Shepherd can't go on playing for ever, Alastair Hignell is going into teaching and I have to admit, too, there have been differences with one or two players at the way things should be done.' That was hardly the stuff of sensation. Heaven knows what the more scurrilous tabloids would have made of it.

I do not blame Graham Russell for running the story. As a journalist he had a job to do, but I also wanted my side of the story to be heard. It was particularly galling to have to wait another day, as I had scored a career-best 145 on that Monday and it seemed so unfair that the news of my departure could not coincide with a good performance for Gloucestershire. Perhaps I was naïve in being frank about my unhappiness, but I had brooded long and hard about it, and felt a great sense of relief when it had all come out. In the dressing-room on the Tuesday morning I had the feeling that my team-mates were grateful that someone had actually spoken out at last, but I was ill-prepared for the storm that broke later that day.

The Cricket Committee met, and while we launched a run chase on the final afternoon it was announced that I had been banned for the rest of the season. Don Perry said they had taken grave exception to my remarks about the absence of the England selectors and to my deteriorating relationship with certain team-mates. He said it was a pity I had chosen such a time to make my views known, but it was he who had changed the date of the statement. The Committee also claimed my comments constituted a breach of contract and that the matter would be referred to the Test and County Cricket Board who might take disciplinary action against me. That never happened.

I was hurt that it had all been blown out of proportion and appalled when it was suggested that I had been sacked. On that final afternoon one of the stewards, Tony Taylor, announced in a stentorian voice, 'Oh, Chris has been sacked!' His words echoed all over the members' area at the ground and I leaned over the balcony and said to him, 'That's not true, Tony, I've been banned for the rest of the season.' Tony replied, 'If it's in the paper that you've been sacked, Chris, it must be true!' I was very embarrassed. The term 'sacked' is a very emotive one and I felt I had to do something to clear my name. I thought of my father who was looking forward to watching me at Bristol now that he had retired. As a former Committee man he would have to sit and listen to all the ill-informed comments about his son being a trouble-maker, how his ambitions had driven him on to unfair criticism of his team-mates. When the headline in the following morning's *Western Daily Press* announced 'Batsman Broad Gets the Sack' I had to do something. My solicitor advised me it would be fruitless to sue the paper and suggested I should get David Collier to sort it out. The next day's edition carried a statement from David Collier that put the record straight: 'We had already agreed to release him from his contract at his own request. But in view of his comments in the press it was merely decided not to pick him for the remainder of the season, which is a very different thing.' David had been as good as his word, and it was typical of him that when it was announced a month later that I had signed for Nottingham-shire he sent me this telegram: *Congratulations on signing for Nottinghamshire. We wish both yourself and Carole every success and happiness for the future. Good luck.*

I still feel sad that I could not have left in a civilized and sensible manner. Every county has at least one discontented established player on its books. I know it came as a severe shock to many followers of Gloucestershire to hear about alleged unrest in the dressing-room, but it was never as serious as that. It was simply a case of a capped player wanting a fresh challenge, to get away from the cosy family environment and see if he could adapt to different wickets. If he did manage the transition, he would hope that improved form would bring him to the attention of the England selectors, especially as the players with South African connections were banned for another year and a half. I do not accept the bulk of the responsibility for the way that scenario was distorted and things got out of hand. A year later I was still reading press articles which began, 'Chris Broad, sacked by Gloucestershire in controversial circumstances. . . .' I took the gravest excep-tion to the breakdown in communication that led to my controversial departure. I must also stress that relations were still very good with most of my team-mates, that I did not consider myself a trouble-maker, even though I was annoyed occasionally by my attitude at times during my final season. Yet the professional who does not have a sulk or lose his temper at times is indeed a paragon – and there are very few of them around in my experience.

People often ask me if I would have stayed at Bristol if a crystal ball had allowed me to visualize their improvement in recent seasons. The answer is no: I had to leave, I needed to test myself elsewhere, in totally different circumstances. I am genuinely delighted for my old county, pleased that David Graveney managed to get through all those distressing votes of no confidence and critical petitions. That cannot have helped his confidence, nor his belief in his ability as cricketer and captain, but he showed great character to come through. After my first season at Trent Bridge, David wrote a thoughtful letter to me, congratulating me on my England début, consoling me about missing the tour to India, and apologizing if he was directly responsible for my departure from Bristol. He wrote:

> 'Many ill-informed people believe there to be some sort of bitter feud between the two of us. Neither did I instigate this or believe it to be true. Of course our views have differed in the past and you can say with justification that my somewhat depressing view of matters at certain stages of the season did not help you or the rest of the team. However, I have attempted to learn from those experiences and accept the realization that it is important to try and remain on an even keel rather than take yours and everybody else's problems upon yourself.'

I was glad for David's and the club's sake that he was coming to terms with the captaincy and that the team started to blossom. The Club started to make some shrewd signings like Bill Athey, Jeremy Lloyds and Courtney Walsh, but the best was Brian Davison. I have always had a great admiration for the positive attitude of Davo and I believe he helped David Graveney a great deal in making things happen on the pitch by will-power and a driving desire to succeed. The Bristol wicket improved – much more pace and bounce to help Walsh and David Lawrence – and hopefully the days of the slow turner have gone for ever. Confidence is so important to professional sportsmen, and in recent seasons the Gloucestershire boys have looked as if they expect to win a few games. Once you have the deep desire to win, you are on the way to success.

I would like to think that my departure may have acted as something of a catalyst at Bristol. Certainly matters were brought more out into the open and David Collier's vision and efficiency became more influential. My good wishes for the welfare of Gloucestershire CCC have always been sincere, even if I know I did the right thing by leaving.

5

1984: A Year of Contrasts

It did not take very long for me to decide where I was going to spend the 1984 season. Both Lancashire and Worcestershire were kind enough to offer me contracts but I liked the idea of playing for Nottinghamshire. They were a successful outfit – the Championship in 1981, the Benson and Hedges Final in 1982 – and I greatly admired their two overseas all-rounders, Clive Rice and Richard Hadlee. There was a vacancy at the top of the order alongside Tim Robinson, and I must have impressed them in making that 145 in my final game for Gloucestershire. Way back in 1977 I had played alongside Tim Robinson for the National Association of Young Cricketers against the Young Australians and we got on straight away. I felt we could be good for each other as opening partners.

Thoughts of an England place were nowhere in my mind as I reported for duty at Trent Bridge in April 1984. I was simply looking forward to a new challenge in another part of the country with a new set of colleagues. The reputation of the Trent Bridge wickets did not bother me – anything would be preferable to grinding out boring runs at bounceless

Bristol – and I was ready to adapt to the extra pace and lift. For a few years the county circuit had been full of lurid tales about the Trent Bridge greentops, but in truth they were beginning to ease by the time I got there. They had been at their most testing in 1981–2, but recently they have become flatter and slower. There is still a fair amount of bounce there, which suits a batsman like me who likes to use the pace of the wicket to nudge the ball around, but it is no longer the county game's horror strip.

It felt right as soon as I walked into Trent Bridge. The players pulled my leg about turning up in jeans, tee shirt, black trainers and thick jumper, only to be told 'You'll get fined' – I had no idea about the required standard of dress. That broke the ice and I felt like a square peg going into a square hole. They seemed good lads, they were bubbling, they expected to enjoy themselves on and off the field. Exactly my sentiments. I was impressed by the facilities of a Test match ground. From the first day of pre-season training you could get into an outdoor net if the weather was kind enough, so a Nottinghamshire player could never blame a poor start to his season on inadequate facilities.

One other thing impressed me. At the start of my first summer we were all invited into the Committee Room and informed that we were welcome to go in there every home Saturday at close of play. We were told we could discuss anything we wished with the Committee, in private if necessary. The avenues for discussion have always been open at Trent Bridge in my time there. To me everything at Trent Bridge seemed geared to success, and I had no doubts that my career would benefit accordingly.

When I look back on the year of 1984 I am amazed that so much happened in such a short space of time. I became a father for the first time, we moved house, I played for England just two months after starting with a new county, I contrived to miss out on the tour to India after scoring 86 in my last Test innings, my county lost out on the Championship by one solitary boundary, and I aggravated an injury that will leave me with an artificial hip in middle age. Truly a roller-coaster of emotions, but I am certain that the low points of that summer have matured me for the better. Although I cursed my ill-fortune at the end of the season, I now realize that I was lucky to get into the England side in the first place.

At the start of the season I felt in very good nick. The winter with Takapuna in New Zealand had gone very well indeed and I returned with a host of trophies and a new daughter, Gemma. Life was satisfying and Tim Robinson and I soon started to compile big partnerships. In the opening first-class game we put on 161 and an undefeated 220 against Oxford University, and I got a hundred – I do like their bowlers! Strange that I was not to score another first-class hundred that summer after 23 April, but I did miss several first-class matches due to England calls and I got my fair share of 50s. Tim Robinson and I continued to do well together in all competitions – 67 against Yorkshire in the John Player League, 148 against Derbyshire in the Benson and Hedges Cup, and 104 against Gloucestershire in the Championship, which pleased me somewhat. The combination of a left-hander and right-hander seemed to unsettle the bowlers' line, and we quickly established that intimate understanding that all successful opening partnerships need. We also had a healthy rivalry right from the start: I wanted to be the man still out in the middle when Tim was dismissed and I am sure he felt the same way. That season Tim was a model of consistency. He played very straight, picking up his runs with controlled driving and deliberate legside placements. I had great respect for his ability and his professional approach to the job in hand.

During the first few weeks of the season I was only concerned with establishing myself at Trent Bridge and striving to improve my batting. Thoughts of an England place just did not occur to me. My first inkling came at the end of May as I sat next to John Wright during our match against Derbyshire. John commiserated with me about not making the England squad for the one-day series against the West Indies, and I was surprised to hear such encouragement from an experienced Test opener. A fortnight earlier I had scored a hundred against Derbyshire in the Benson and Hedges Cup but, although I did play well, the attack was hardly in the West Indian class. In any event, both Graeme Fowler and Andy Lloyd did well in the one-day internationals and they deserved to be picked for the start of the Test series.

In a sense, Malcolm Marshall is the man to thank for getting me into the England side. If he had not felled Andy Lloyd with that sickening blow to the temple early in the First Test, I might not have got in all summer. At the time Andy was looking very composed and I am sure that he would have had at least another chance after Edgbaston. Andy deserved to be in the team through sheer weight of runs at county level, and any opener who got 50 against those West Indians would rightly be rewarded with a vote of confidence from the selectors. I have often thought that Andy Lloyd and I are similar players, quite apart from being left-handers, and if the luck had gone his way there was no reason why he would not have become an England regular and I might have missed out for good. Better openers than I have been disappointed over the years.

The news that I was selected to play for England was broken to me in the dining-room at Leicester by the England captain himself. David Gower came over to me, tapped me on the shoulder, and said, 'Congratulations, you're in.' I genuinely did not know what he was talking about till he explained. Then I rushed out, looking for Carole who was just unpacking the car. 'Guess where I'm playing next Thursday?' I asked. It took some time for it to sink in to both of us, and the champagne that night tasted very sweet indeed. An England début at Lord's, of all places!

Of course the press jumped to the glib assumption that my England call-up stemmed from a change of county. They forgot that many good openers were still banned, and therefore the cupboard was not exactly bulging with options. They ignored the fact that the selectors clearly felt left-handers were needed against the West Indian fast bowlers, on the grounds that they did not bowl a consistently good line against us. The injury to Andy Lloyd was conveniently ignored. I was, after all, in pretty good form – more than 800 first-class runs with an average of more than 50 – and who is to say that I might not have been selected if I was still at Bristol? It is true that my new county was more successful than Gloucestershire, but luck had a great deal to do with my selection.

It was hardly surprising that I got to Lord's an hour before the scheduled time on the eve of the Test. I did not want to waste a moment in enjoying the build-up. It may sound a cliché, but Lord's is a fantastic place and I felt privileged to make my England début there. Everyone wants to play at Lord's, including the established England players: its atmosphere of tradition and history never fails to inspire. To me everything is done properly there. You are not allowed to practise on the field of play: you have to go over to the Nursery End and train – in whites – and when you come back from the nets the atmosphere is really building up. You walk past the square and drink in the awe-inspiring sight of that marvellous old pavilion, standing out like the cliffs of Dover. You go up the steps, past all the members, into those massive dressing-rooms with oceans of room in which to change; you can spread yourself out and there are large baths in which to enjoy a good soak. All this, plus superb food supplied by the redoubtable Nancy, and shortish boundaries. Terrific.

When I walked into the England dressing-room that Wednesday, Geoff Miller was the only one there before me. He congratulated me; I chose a corner where I could be as unobtrusive as possible, walked down to the pavilion's double doors, looked out at the wicket being prepared, and said to myself: 'This is it, I've made it, this will do for me.' All my new colleagues were very supportive and warm to me as they trickled in. Great players like Bob Willis, David Gower and Ian Botham could not have been more generous; I almost reminded Bob Willis that he had once given me his autograph! Then it was over to the nets and I was the centre of media attention: an interview with Peter West for BBC's 'Breakfast Time', camera close-ups of my batting and fielding, and endless quotes for the press. That night, at the team dinner, I met Chairman of Selectors, Peter May. Throughout the meal I sat there, soaking up the unique atmosphere. For the established players it was just a ritual, but for me it was a special occasion.

I slept very poorly that night. I was awake from about three o'clock, far too excited to settle. Down to breakfast about eight o'clock, to join that perennial early riser, Bob Willis. From our window we looked down on the queues already forming and Bob told me, 'Enjoy this, it's the time of your life.' He had already announced his retirement from the game at the end of the season and he knew this was his last Test at Lord's. After breakfast I went back upstairs to put the suit and tie on, and it was time to walk across the road to Lord's. I joined Paul Downton, and while we strolled along, I was aware of all the cricket fans nudging each other, pointing out the new boy. When I found out we were batting first, I was pleased: it seemed appropriate to bat on the first morning. I was signing autograph sheets at the time, but I carried on with it even though the blood was rushing to my cheeks. I needed to do something for a few more minutes to settle my nerves and I felt fine after that. I gave myself about twenty-five minutes to get ready, remembering to put on my left pad first. A final five minutes on my own, determined not to think about the bowlers I would be facing. 'Just play straight and you'll be alright,' I kept telling myself. The good wishes from the rest of the team were very touching and there was a good feeling about the place. Once I knew I was playing that morning, I was handed my England cap, sweater and tie, and when I put the sweater on I remembered Derek Randall's words about how the chest seems to swell an extra couple of inches. As Graeme Fowler and I walked through the Long Room the members applauded us and the noise reverberated all around the ground as we stepped on to the turf. It was a fantastic feeling and I loved sharing it with such a chirpy character. Graeme was great to me, geeing me up after every over and doing his utmost to make me feel confident. As we walked out to the middle we had to pass Joel Garner as he measured out his run-up. Normally a cheerful soul with Somerset, he was stony-faced, concentrating hard. That was to be the pattern throughout with the West Indies: we never saw them socially that summer. Clearly they felt their will to win would be diluted if they mixed with us after close of play.

At the start of my innings I was doubly lucky. Graeme Fowler took most of the early overs from Joel Garner, which gave me time to settle down, while at the other end the new ball was given to Milton Small. He seemed very nervous and he over-pitched a lot; I managed to get three boundaries in a row off him through mid-wicket and I felt very confident. If

Malcolm Marshall had opened instead it would have been a shade different! I was surprised how relaxed I felt, I was loving the big-match atmosphere and the challenge. A nice gesture from David Evans the umpire was appreciated: at the start of my innings he said, 'If it helps you, I'll chat to you when you're not on strike and you do the same to me if you want. But I shan't say a word to you if you want to concentrate.' I was more than happy to chat away to David and I am sure that it helped ease the tension.

I was caught at slip off a no-ball from Marshall and was almost run out by Greenidge, running in from cover – both when I was in the 20s – but apart from that I felt I played as well as possible. We had to go off once or twice for bad light, but that did not hamper my concentration. On the contrary, the sincere encouragement and praise from the lads in the dressing-room boosted my confidence. We put on over 100 and I had reached my 50 when I was out in very annoying circumstances. Marshall often tries to bowl a bouncer second ball of an over, and in his first over of a new spell after tea he did just that. I knew it would be short, but it failed to bounce in the way I anticipated; in the end, I played at it too high, it touched my bottom hand and went through to the wicket-keeper. It was a nothing shot to a nothing delivery after doing all the hard work, but I suppose it was a case of being worn down by the fast bowlers and eventually making a mistake.

At least I had done myself justice and we had given the team a good start. I would have settled for a score of 55 against the best side in the world when play began, and at the close a total of 167 for 2 was very encouraging. After play ended I had another graphic example of the gulf between Test and county cricket when I attended a function organized by a major electrical firm. I came away laden with 'freebies' that I still use to this day, and it was strange to see mature individuals in charge of huge budgets behaving like autograph hunters when England cricketers are around – even novices like me. It was light years away from a quiet pint, leaning up against the bar after a typical day on the county circuit.

I slept like a log that night and then enjoyed the newspaper coverage of the first day. My photograph on the front page of *The Times* was definitely one for the scrapbook! Graeme Fowler reached an admirable hundred and I was delighted for him after his genuine efforts to relax his new partner the day before. Unfortunately my most vivid memory of that second day has nothing to do with the play, engrossing though it was. That evening I was phoning Carole from the hotel foyer and in the process injured my hip. That sounds ridiculous, I know, but as I swivelled to get up from the chair a muscle caught a bone in my hip joint. This had happened to me before and it usually eased after stretching my groin. I tried that exercise that night, but the bone would not go back in. A hot bath failed to relax the muscles and I went to sleep on it, hoping to push it back into place. It was no better the following morning and the England physiotherapist Bernard Thomas gave me treatment with electric pulses before the start of play. He strapped me up as if I had a groin strain but after three-quarters of an hour I was in too much pain and had to leave the field. Bernard took me to a hospital just around the corner and the X-ray was disturbing. The ball and socket joints of the hip were not fitting properly and the prognosis was fairly worrying. I was told that with luck I would get through my career, but that I would probably need an artificial hip later in life. What a thing to tell a young sportsman on his début for his country! Apparently the hip problem had nothing to do with the osteomyelitis of my teens, but that was no consolation.

When we returned to Lord's I had to get ready to bat. Not the best time to go in – no wonder I got nought. Garner pitched one on middle stump and when I played at it the ball was six inches outside the off stump and I was caught at third slip. I was very depressed: in the midst of my elation I had stumbled upon a problem that would always be with me throughout my sporting career. Bernard Thomas showed me some stretching exercises to keep the joint moving, and since then I have had no real problems, but I know it could flare up again. It has never been worse than during my Test début; perhaps the tension of the occasion manifested itself in my body in a mysterious way. That night I turned down the chance of going to Elton John's house for a party and drove up to tell Carole about my injury. I hope that explains my rather stiff movements in the field – I have never been the swiftest mover, and the awareness of the hip problem means that I cannot change direction swiftly lest it goes again.

The hip injury eased for the rest of the Test and I could once again settle down to enjoy the atmosphere. Somehow we contrived to lose a game that we had contested keenly for all but the last four hours. When we asked the West Indies to get 342 in just over five hours there seemed no way it could be anything but a draw. We had no chance of bowling them out on a flat wicket and it seemed the asking rate would be too much for a Test. Gordon Greenidge changed all that. He did not play a false stroke until he had reached 196 when he top-edged a hook over my head at fine leg for six. Then he stood in the middle of the pitch, slamming his pad with his bat, then dabbing at the wicket in anguish. It was so important to Greenidge to get the runs in the right fashion and I really admired the professional way that he unfurled his shots and simply dominated the bowling.

In the end we were thrashed, but that did not lessen my enjoyment of my first Test, apart from my injury. I made nought on my début but it could have been worse: it might have come on that first morning. I told myself that if I had been in a better frame of mind in that second innings I would have played a different stroke to the ball from Garner. Peter May did wonders for my confidence when he said on the first morning, 'Don't worry – whatever happens, you will play in the next Test, so just relax.' I told myself it was a county match, that Garner was playing for Somerset and Marshall for Hampshire. It was good to see Marshall go round the wicket on that first day: that meant we were frustrating him, because he had to alter his line. The short square boundaries were a godsend to a nudger and deflector like me, and it was good to see the ball race away to the fence once it beat the fielder. The tempo of the match also surprised me. A six-hour day compared very favourably indeed with that summer's regulation of at least 117 overs a day in the County Championship. At Lord's we had a great deal of time to move around between overs instead of rushing about, and it really felt a different sort of game.

The next Test at Leeds was an anti-climax compared to Lord's. The crowd was nowhere near as supportive, possibly because there was not one Yorkshire player in the England side. The atmosphere felt flat and there was a distinct air of defeatism in our camp. It was not a good batting wicket and several of us got out to unplayable deliveries. The bounce was very uneven, and against bowlers of their speed and accuracy you had to be very lucky to survive. 'How can you play that?' was the lament offered by many an England player when he returned to the dressing-room, and I have some sympathy for that feeling. In the second innings, with the wicket deteriorating, I got a ball from Marshall that I just had to play: it got up off a length and flicked the edge of my bat. Against someone of his pace there was no chance of getting out of the way. We had nobody of his speed, and our fast-medium bowlers could be avoided or fended off because their batsmen had extra precious seconds to adjust.

My first innings in the Leeds Test was typical of my efforts for England that summer. I got a start, then got out for 32, just like the old days with Gloucestershire when my concentration would let me down. Somehow I just could not stay in and make it count after doing all the hard work. I had seen off Marshall, Garner and Holding but got out to the undemanding off-spin of Roger Harper, trying to cut a ball that bounced rather more than I expected and top-edging a catch to slip. Infuriating. There was one consolation from my innings, though: it seemed as if I had effectively put Malcolm Marshall out of the game. On the first morning I edged a ball to him in the gully and after it bounced a couple of times it hit him on the left thumb. It turned out to be a double fracture and we all thought, 'Oh good, he won't be bowling anymore in this Test.' We were wrong – he came out in the second innings, took 7 for 53 and, with his thumb heavily plastered, even took a caught-and-bowled to dismiss Fowler. He also batted number eleven, in obvious discomfort, to enable Larry Gomes to reach his century.

That effort by Marshall was typical of the West Indies' performances in 1984. We were no match for their collective professionalism, the way their best players maintained pride in their performance. At Leeds we were only 32 behind on first innings, but soon we were 13 for 2 and struggling. Fowler and Gower got us to 104 for 2, but then Marshall broke through to leave us 135 for 6 on Saturday night, with the match lost. The pressure from their fast bowlers was relentless, compounded by our awareness that nothing less than a big stand for every wicket would give us a chance of even drawing the game. On the rare occasions when the fast men were rested, Harper would nip in with his off-spin and he would clean up as we relaxed.

It was a demoralized England dressing-room on that Saturday night and we had a day and a half to contemplate our third defeat in a row. We subsided gently on the Monday, with the tail folding, and then we dropped a few catches when we had a chance to discomfit them on such an unreliable wicket. My only personal satisfaction from the Leeds Test came when I took my first catch for England – Baptiste off Allott at wide mid-off. If I say so myself, it was a useful effort: high to my left, not my best side for catching. I was grateful to Ian Botham for a nice gesture after that, because he made a bee-line for me to congratulate me on my first catch while everyone else went straight to the bowler. Botham's thoughtful gestures are often missed by those who are set on denigrating him.

We needed more than just thoughtful gestures from Botham when we assembled for the Old Trafford Test. He and the senior players just had to start turning in great performances if we were to avoid a 5–0 thrashing in the series. That awful prospect was beginning to loom and every newspaper was reminding us about it. Yet Old Trafford was the most dispiriting of our efforts against the West Indies that summer. We had them 70 for 4 on the first day, but Jeff Dujon and Gordon Greenidge rallied them. That was fair enough, they were both fine players, but then Winston Davis came in as night-watchman and helped Greenidge add no less than 170 precious runs. Whatever confidence we had drained out of us. I epitomized that lack of confidence when I ought to have made a better fist at a possible catch offered by Davis when he was in the 40s. The ball was hit out to me at deep mid-wicket but I could not make up my mind whether or not to go for it. I was too worried about looking a fool if I dropped it, and I allowed it to land near me and took it on the first bounce. It was a negative response from a player in a team that was now thinking negatively. Two years later, in

Australia, I was going for harder chances than that one and catching them.

When the West Indies made 500 we all knew our number was up. Before the start we had noticed cracks in the wicket and you could put your boot on an area of grass and it would move. Against their fast bowlers we would simply not know what the ball would be doing. The outfield was not in the best of nick, with long strands of grass and the surface bleached by the drought. It would be a nightmare for the outfielders, yet somehow we instinctively knew that our opponents would still look superior to us. We just drifted through that Test, without proper direction. The incident when we failed to avoid the follow-on summed it all up. I was at the other end when Paul Terry suffered a broken arm from a ball by Davis. The ball was short, he was not in the right position, and Paul simply braced himself for the impact. I shall never forget the sickening thud as ball struck forearm, and poor Paul was led away. Later he had to go out and bat when the ninth wicket fell; we needed another 23 to avoid following on and Allan Lamb was still there, 98 not out. I was sitting on the players' balcony when Norman Cowans was out and we all thought that was the end of our innings. The players started trooping off, and then suddenly Paul Terry walked out on to the pitch. We were equally surprised because there was no sign of David Gower – he was in the captain's room – and Allan Lamb was looking vainly up at us for guidance. Paul Terry could easily have been 'timed out' since more than two minutes had elapsed since the dismissal of Cowans, but it became even more ludicrous when he got to the wicket. Lamb played the first five balls of the next over defensively, then flicked Holding to fine leg. He ran a single and it seemed that he had sensibly decided that the only way to get the next 22 runs was for him to take the strike. Suddenly he decided to go for the second run to fine leg and he scrambled home to complete his century. Then Lamb started to walk towards the pavilion, under the mistaken impression that Terry had been sent out there purely to help him get his century. In the process Terry had been exposed to Garner's new over, with his left arm in a sling under his sweater! Predictably he lasted two balls and we had to follow on.

It was muddled thinking and a classic example of individual needs taking precedence over the team's overall aim. It was far more important to avoid the follow-on than for Allan Lamb to get his hundred, and in any case he would have managed that easily if he had somehow gathered another 23 runs while protecting Terry. He might have failed – especially against their attack – but at least he should have been seen to try that strategy. Compare the way Marshall supported Gomes for a 12-run stand in the previous Test, as Gomes got his hundred. Once again, we had failed to be seen to take the right option and one can imagine the frame of mind of Messrs Broad and Fowler as they prepared to bat again. As we had no idea what was going on, we did not have those precious extra minutes to prepare ourselves mentally to go out and face the best fast bowling line-up in the world. As a result Fowler was bowled by Holding immediately for nought and we had our backs to the wall right away. By the close of that fourth day we were 120 for 5, with Harper taking four of the wickets. He got me lbw and I was furious. Some sections of the press commented that I seemed upset at Don Oslear's decision, but that was rubbish. Harper was bowling from round the wicket, and just as he let the ball go a waitress came out of the executive boxes behind his arm and started walking down the steps. I just could not pull away quickly enough and I was mesmerized. All I could do was pad up without playing a shot and I was plumb out. I gave the executive boxes, not Don Oslear, a filthy look. In that split second I should have pulled away and let the ball hit my stumps while apologizing to the bowler.

An innings defeat was no more than we deserved. The West Indies had been let out of jail on the first two days and we had not made it difficult enough for them as they surged to victory. There seemed no tactical pattern, no coherent strategy. Consider our dressing-room during one of the many breaks for bad light on the second day. Greenidge and Davis were frustrating us out on the field during their long stand and we needed to get at least the night-watchman out. After we trooped off for bad light Botham and Fowler started larking around in our dressing-room and soon lumps of sugar, cakes and even pad whitening were flying around. There were no selectors present and the captain was in his own room, so no one could tell them to stop it. I wonder if the radio and television commentaries at that time were hazarding guesses at our discussions while we had a tactical regrouping?

When we reassembled at the Oval I sensed a mood of determination. No one fancied being part of a 5–0 whitewash and we knew that the faster, truer Oval wicket would give us a chance to bowl them out and at least bat in reasonable conditions without fear of getting any limbs broken. On the first day we did well to bowl them out for 190, although they again showed their resilience to recover from 70 for 6. By the close I was out to a delivery from Joel Garner that still haunts me: it pitched outside leg stump, cut back to move away from me at speed, and cannoned into my off-stump via my left pad. I stood up, cursed to myself, and thought, 'How the hell can he make the ball move that much?' and I am grateful that my career has not suffered from too many deliveries like that one.

Next day my colleagues had a torrid time as Marshall went beyond the bounds of fair play. Pat Pocock frustrated him as

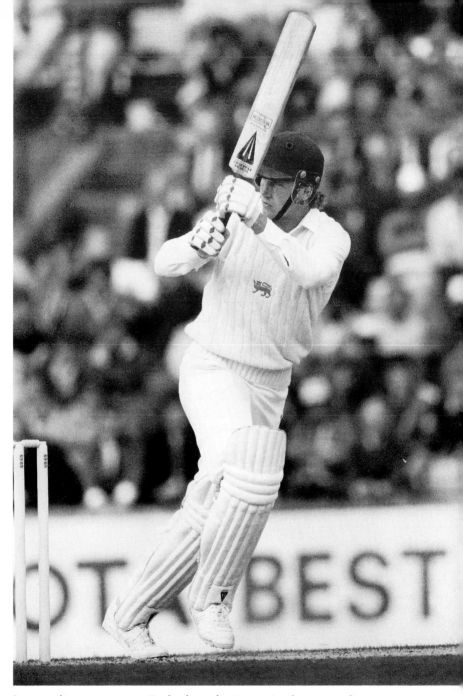

It was a pleasure to wear an England one-day international sweater at home
for the first time – although getting out for 99 against Pakistan
in this game at the Oval in May 1987 was a shade frustrating.
I would have settled for 99 though at the start of my innings!

One year old: was I trying to find the cricket commentary on the radio?

The Broad youngsters: *from left to right*
Michael (aged $5\frac{1}{2}$), Wendy (one year old) and myself (aged $3\frac{1}{2}$).
My brother Michael was to die tragically young in 1982 of a massive heart attack.

My other great sporting passion has always been rugby.
Here I am in 1974 pictured in my school's 1st XV.

Early days on the Gloucestershire staff.

Two moments from the 1982 season with Gloucestershire –
(*below*) playing one of my favourite shots off my legs against Yorkshire and
(*above*) surviving a close shave against Middlesex,
with Paul Downton and Clive Radley in attendance.

Two glimpses of my technique:
(*left*) the bread-and-butter steer
through the offside that gets me
many useful singles, and (*above*)
the avoidance of the short-pitched
delivery. My England team-mate
Neil Foster has tried me out with a
bouncer, but I will not be tempted.
A long time ago I worked out that
the hook was not a percentage shot
for me, so the fast bowler can tire
himself out as long as he wants.
After all, there are enough ways
to get yourself out.

Leeds, 1984, and Malcolm Marshall
has dismissed me for just two
in the second innings.
Despite a double fracture of
the left thumb, Marshall still
took 7 for 53 in this innings.

Yes, England cricketers do read
the newspapers, especially if
they have done well the day before.
After my first day of Test cricket
at Lord's in 1984, I read every
word about my half-century
that Fleet Street had to offer.

Part of the demoralized England team on the Old Trafford balcony
during the Test against the West Indies in 1984. We are heading
for another heavy defeat, and our expressions tell it all:
(*from left to right*) our captain David Gower, myself, Norman Cowans,
Graeme Fowler, Paul Terry (his left arm broken by a bouncer from Winston
Davis) and Nick Cook.

Battling away against the off-spin of Roger Harper during the 1984 series
that was dominated by West Indian fast bowling.
Jeff Dujon is waiting for any mistakes behind the stumps.

Even in the tensest situations, I always try to have a laugh on the field.
David Constant is one of those umpires who agrees.

The Broad family – wife Carole, daughter Gemma and son Stuart,
who was born in the week I collected my 'pair' at Leicester.
After that my form blossomed and I forced my way back into
the England side. Perhaps Stuart is my lucky mascot!

he hung around for the first forty-five minutes of the day and he received some brutal, short-pitched deliveries that some pundits felt ought to have been stopped. Marshall only had himself to blame for getting frustrated, because such a great bowler knows more than enough about the art to dismiss someone like Pocock. Line and length, not short-pitched stuff aimed at the body, was all that was needed. Pocock had no complaints, but David Constant was criticized by the media for failing to speak to either bowler or captain. It was just one more example of the West Indies' obsession in wiping us out for a clean sweep.

For a time at the Oval we had a good chance of victory, but as always someone would come along and turn the tide against us. This time it was Desmond Haynes who had struggled all series. He chose the vital innings to get a hundred after they had started badly. The bowlers backed him up with useful scores and we were left to get 375 in ten hours. I genuinely felt we could at least get somewhere near that target, and I was so upset when we lost an early wicket. Chris Tavaré and I then kept them out for nearly three hours and their heads started to droop a little. I had noticed that tendency in my first innings at Lord's when they were very quiet as Fowler and I added a hundred, and the feeling nagged away that the West Indies could get very down and depressed if things were not going their way. Just as Tavaré and I were getting on top, Michael Holding changed the game's course. He came on for a new spell and I settled down in my stance, ready for him. That summer he had come in off a shortened run, because he had been troubled by various injuries, but when I looked up I was amazed to see he had gone back twice as far. He had suddenly decided to come in off his old, long run. I was mesmerized, watching him glide in from thirty-five yards away, and the ball was on me so quickly. It was a bouncer; I lost sight of it, it flicked my glove to gully and I was on my way. I could not believe that someone with such a smooth approach to the wicket could bowl so fast. Holding must have been an absolute terror earlier in his career, but he has since compensated for any lack of pace with supreme tactical intelligence. On this occasion I had too much time to think about him as he ran in and that was fatal.

Holding got three of us out that evening in seventeen balls and we were again doomed to come second. It was a great tribute to Ian Botham's reputation that the papers and public still thought we had a chance on the final morning, with 5 wickets to fall and 200 needed. But the West Indians had done their homework on Botham: they did not give him much to drive throughout the series, and they pitched it short to get him hooking in the air. They knew that he was not the kind of man to hang around just accumulating, like a Broad or a Tavaré, and they consistently bowled in the right place to him. They also worked out where to bowl at me after Milton Small suffered at my hands in my first innings. I still got a few legside boundaries thereafter, but nowhere near as many opportunities in my favourite area.

With Botham out after a brief show of defiance, it was all over within an hour and the 'blackwash' (as one banner quaintly put it) was complete. That was the cue for a frightening invasion of the pitch, during which Jonathan Agnew lost his gloves, helmet, bat and arm protector. He was in tears by the time he got back to the safety of the dressing-room, and to make matters worse we had to stand beside the unruly hordes on the pitch as the presentations were made. It was unfair to the players, especially the English ones as we were taunted by the gleeful West Indian supporters. It left a sour taste in the mouth, although the opposition players were sympathetic and friendly enough.

For the first time that series they invited us up to their dressing-room for a drink and most of us went there. They had worked very hard indeed to attain their target and we all had to admire their dedication, even down to avoiding us socially during the series. Clive Lloyd had a marvellous way of getting the best out of his team and they were an instructive lesson in the way they went about their pre-match training. All the superstars were expected to go through a rigorous session each morning before play started, and they looked an integrated, efficient, athletic group. We should have tried to look equally positive, even if they were superior to us when play started. I felt that the public ought to have seen us training hard together rather than drifting around lethargically. No matter how prestigious the player, he cannot afford to give the public or media any ammunition, especially when we were always going to be on the wrong end of a few defeats from the best team around. We were, after all, in the shop window, and for someone like myself, who loved the Test match scene, it was disappointing to see such passive acceptance of the fates from our top players. It was not up to the younger players to pull the ship round, the inspiration had to come from the experienced, class performers – but at no stage did we talk about our bowling or fielding strategy at the pre-Test dinners. Peter May would stand up and tell us we were the best available men to represent England and that we had it in us to make it hard for the opposition, but no one would get down to basics like where to bowl at Viv Richards or how we could possibly combat their fast bowlers. The feeling seemed to be 'Oh, there's another Test coming up in a fortnight, we'll try to get it right then.' We simply did not make things happen, and when I saw their bowlers make runs and field so superbly I thought of Mike Procter's dictum in 1979 that every professional cricketer should be able to be versatile. The casual, world-weary attitude of the senior England players disappointed me. Perhaps they had played too much cricket. Certainly Ian Botham was jaded: in the

Lord's Test he never left his couch in the dressing-room when we were batting, apart from walking out to bat. He would sit there watching television, eating his lunch or tea, and just pick up his bat and walk out when it was his turn. He did not seem as concerned at our poor performances as others in the team. He was totally different when I toured with him in Australia; perhaps that 1984 summer was the lowest ebb in his Test career.

We should not have lost 5–0. At least two games ought to have been drawn, but in the end too many England players seemed to accept that the great West Indian fast bowlers would wear us down. As for myself, I loved playing for England but wished I had fared better. Getting fifty in my first innings was a great start, but I then got out far too often when set. I got a few runs each Test which ensured I would hang on for another chance. After scoring just 4 and 39 at the Oval I was concerned that I might be dropped for the Sri Lanka Test, because I ought to have scored more runs on a good batting wicket and fast outfield. Yet David Gower put my mind at ease when we languished in the bath together during the Oval Test. He moved into a squatting position in the bath, with his heels resting on the floor, and he said to me, 'This is a position you'll have to get used to over the winter in India.' I did not know exactly what he meant, but the implication was clear – I would be touring India with England a few months later. That improved my morale and I looked forward to boosting my confidence against the Sri Lankans. That experience was to have the reverse effect.

For the next two years I kept wondering who was the last player to score 86 in a Test and never represent his country again. I owe the spectators who came to Lord's on that Saturday a heck of a lot, because I must have been awful to watch. It is true that getting a big score was uppermost in my mind: I felt one major innings would ensure my selection for the India tour and I was petrified at getting out against a fairly friendly bowling attack. My performance summed up England's display in this Test. We had been expected to hammer the Sri Lankans out of sight after the traumas against the West Indians, but they batted superbly on a flat Lord's pitch. After two days, the first priority was to avoid the follow-on: that would have been the last straw for England's supporters after all the previous disasters, and I set out my stall to get a big score and in the process guide us to safety. Not a glamorous objective, I admit, but as a team we were thinking negatively by then. I believe those England players who had gone through the whole summer simply wanted to avoid another ignominious defeat, get through the game and look forward to a few weeks' rest in the autumn.

Graeme Fowler and I got off to a healthy start, but when Chris Tavaré and I came together things just ground to a halt. Poor Tav had had a mediocre season and his confidence was very low. There had been talk about the England vice-captaincy for the winter tour, but first he just had to get some runs to justify his place in the side. We were both in the same boat and we played dreadfully. Between lunch and tea we made 49 runs in 27 overs and the hoots of derision were very embarrassing and well-deserved. I genuinely had no idea we had scored so few, but we had made little attempt to pick up short singles or pressurize the bowlers. By then I had got used to the slower tempo of Tests and was simply waiting for the runs to come along, but I agree that Tav and I ought to have had a chat together and push on. At tea David Gower had a quiet word and, when Tav was out, he came in and creamed the ball around in his inimitable style, which only made me feel worse. The only bowler who really taxed me was D. S. de Silva, the leg-spinner, and I at least had some consolation from struggling through against a good spinner and being undefeated at the close.

That night the captain apologized to the press for our turgid batting and he was absolutely right. It was not a situation for a percentage batsman like me, but I owed it to the spectators to have tried to dominate the undemanding bowling. When I was out on the Monday morning – playing a weak, wafting shot to be caught behind – I was relieved. I did not deserve a hundred, although in the light of subsequent events I have often wondered what might have happened if I had got those extra fourteen runs. On the Monday evening I was having a drink in the Cornhill tent when a pressman came up to me and said, 'I've got this awful feeling you may have batted yourself out of the tour.' I was amazed. Admittedly it had been a pretty poor exhibition, but surely good judges knew by now that I was capable of a good deal more. After all, I had just got my highest Test score and 86 is not a bad effort when you have played badly. It is true I had been thinking primarily of my own interests as I batted on and on, but international sides are full of players with that single-minded attitude. Surely the selectors would take those factors into account when they picked the tour party?

After that chat I was dreading having to bat a second time in the Test and I was secretly pleased that the Sri Lankans kept us in the field all day. I just could not afford a failure and hoped that an innings of 86 would be enough. Those five days had done nothing for England's tarnished image, and we were all glad when it was over. In five Tests I had averaged 31, a reasonable return when you consider that I had earned my spurs against the West Indies. At that stage in the season, I would have bet on a place for me in the tour party – but the words of foreboding in the Cornhill tent kept recurring.

For the time being, my attention was concentrated on helping Nottinghamshire win the Championship title. We had three games to go when I returned from Test duty. No problems with the first – Northants were beaten by an innings inside two days. If we had beaten Sussex in the next match the Championship would have been ours, because we were ahead of Essex on bowling points, but John Barclay did us no favours with his declaration and we ended up with a draw. We went on to Taunton for the last game, knowing that victory would win us the title, no matter what Essex achieved up at Old Trafford. We arrived at the hotel on the Friday night to find that we had been booked into rooms immediately above the area where a rock band played until the early hours of the morning, so our preparation for the big game was hardly satisfactory. Nevertheless we decided to enjoy the match and not get too tense about the next few days. That was the right attitude because we had enough good players to get us through if we played to our full potential.

All the drama happened on the final day. Essex had already beaten Lancashire in two days, so they were gathered at the county's headquarters in Chelmsford, anxiously waiting to see how we would fare. If we beat Somerset the Championship was ours. Ian Botham's declaration – 297 in 60 overs – was a very fair one because he kept the spinners on for all but 8 of those overs. Many another captain would have just shut the door but Botham's good sportsmanship ensured that we would deserve the title if we won at Taunton. Tim Robinson and I got us off to a good start and Clive Rice played superbly until he was caught at deep mid-wicket off a full toss. That proved to be the crucial wicket, even though the support batters all did well. With three overs left we needed 36. Young Andy Pick managed to get a few in the middle of the bat and ran well as his senior partner, Mike Bore, struck out for glory. The young slow-left-arm spinner Stephen Booth began the last over with 14 needed for the title and 1 wicket in hand. Mike Bore hit marvellously well to pick up 10 off the first three balls, by which time we were ecstatic in the dressing-room. Then Mike started thinking about what was at stake and missed the next ball. The tension got to him, he launched himself at the fifth ball and it spiralled away in the direction of long on. 'That's it, we've won!' we all shouted, but we had not spotted the figure of Richard Ollis out on the long-off boundary. He ran round and took the catch safely and the title went to Essex by a matter of yards.

When he returned to the dressing-room Andy Pick burst into tears and Mike Bore just stared straight ahead of him. He had won us the Northants game with his bowling, and after doing all the hard work with the bat at Taunton he had failed at the last gasp. I felt desperately sorry for him and for all of us. It must have been a terribly long drive back to Nottingham that night and there was little consolation for us in a great game of cricket.

I was staying on in the West Country to play in a benefit match for Ian Botham the following night, so I motored up to Bristol that evening to stay with Carole and my parents. An important day in my career loomed the next day – the England tour party was to be announced.

The moment when I discovered I was not selected will stay vividly in my mind for all time. The Broads had gone to have lunch with the Bainbridges and we had been joined by Andy Brassington and his wife. We switched on the radio news at eleven o'clock and it was announced that three uncapped players were going. Nothing else except their names: Chris Cowdrey, Martyn Moxon and Tim Robinson. Immediately I blurted out, 'I'm not in then,' and Phil Bainbridge said, 'Don't worry, they haven't read out the whole team.' Yet I knew that the presence of Moxon and Robinson would mean no room for me, because Fowler would not be dropped after his brave efforts that summer. Phil phoned up BBC Radio Bristol and the team was read out to him. I was out. We went to a pub for lunch and I have no idea what I said or who talked to me. Clearly I was dreadful, morose company that lunchtime, but I know everyone understood. The doleful forecast of that pressman kept returning to me: 'I've got this awful feeling you may have batted yourself out of the tour.' Perhaps I had made it too obvious that I was playing for my place in the tour party, perhaps they thought that my long battle against de Silva had not inspired confidence for the encounters with the Indian spinners. Someone murmured that I would have been better off injured and out of the Sri Lanka Test, but I could not accept that: I needed one more big innings that summer in a Test and I had got it. It was a very long afternoon.

By the time I got to Taunton that evening to play for Ian Botham I was more philosophical. I would battle back, score hundreds of runs, and they would not then ignore me. Tony Brown, Somerset's Secretary and the appointed Indian tour manager, told me that I was not even in the running at the selection meeting. It did not even come to a vote between me, Moxon or Robinson. That did little for my morale and I started to brood on the injustice of announcing the tour party on the radio before a disappointed player can be personally contacted. It seems nobody knew where to find me on that Wednesday for a quiet word, but Tony Brown, the tour manager, knew I would be in the area that day because I was due to play for his county captain. A call to my parents' home in Bristol would have gleaned the necessary contact. A week later I was playing in a benefit match for Wayne Daniel and David Gower was also in attendance. After Gordon Greenidge had said to him 'How can you leave him out after he's scored 86?', he pulled me aside and apologized for the lack of prior warning. He had tried to ring me at home, and did not know where to find me. There was no mention of his conversation with me in the bath at the Oval during the West Indies Test. I do understand it is difficult to draw the line between near-misses and no-hopers when the captain of a touring side wants to offer a word of consolation to the disappointed player, but I would suggest that some communication with a man who had played for England throughout that summer was desirable.

The selection of my county partner was absolutely right and I felt so at the time. He had scored over 2,000 runs and to me he had the solid, strong temperament to do well at Test level. We met up a week or so after the tour party was announced. We were playing in a double-wicket competition at Trent Bridge and he walked in as I was changing. I called out, 'Congrats, Robbo – well done!' and I genuinely meant it. Tim looked embarrassed and moved away into his usual area of the dressing-room. We have never since talked about it and I am not sure if we ever will, because it is all too personal. Perhaps we might chew it over if we ever establish ourselves as England's opening pair, but until then we keep our personal thoughts to ourselves.

That September I eventually consoled myself with two considerations. First, that no one has a divine right to play for England, that men like Peter Willey and David Steele had missed out on a tour to India after taking the West Indies flak. I was not the first to suffer, nor would I be the last. The selectors were perfectly entitled to adopt a 'horses for courses' policy. Secondly, I had achieved much in the twelve months that had elapsed since the sad break with Gloucestershire. It had been a hectic period and I had thoroughly enjoyed the vast majority of it. I would do all I could to get back in the England team. Little did I know that another twenty-six months and twenty-two Tests would slip by before the call came again.

6

1985: A Year of Frustration

I should have got away from cricket in England during the winter of 1984–5, but I made the great mistake of working in the marketing department at Trent Bridge. This is not meant to sound ungrateful to David Seward, our Marketing Manager; he was on the phone very quickly and asked if I had thought of anything to do that winter. When he asked me to take the place of Tim Robinson in the office I had a quiet chuckle and thought, 'Why not? It'll be good experience, another string to my bow.' It was the worst thing I could have done. People kept either consoling me for missing out on the tour or remarking on Robbo's marvellous performances out there. Now I was delighted for my opening partner, a player I rated very highly, but I just could not escape the feeling that I could also be out there with him, piling up huge scores on flat wickets, compared to ducking the thunder and lightning of Marshall, Garner and Holding. Nothing personal, simply an honest professional assessment, laced with a dash of justifiable envy. Every morning of that Indian Test series, the radio commentaries would blare out the glad tidings in our office. It got on my nerves and I should not have been there.

Self-pity is not an attractive character trait, especially in a grown man with a young daughter, and Carole kept telling me to snap out of it. The thought kept coming back that I could have been doing even better than Robbo, given the chance. I did not know Martyn Moxon at all – I had hardly seen him play – but I was very unreasonable about him as I sat at home, brooding. I hope people will understand it was simply a human reaction, with no malice intended. Quite simply, I needed to pour out my heart to another cricketer who had suffered a similar rebuff or, failing that, to be abroad making hundreds in some form of cricket to prove I could still play the game. Looking back on it now, it was a good exercise in character-building. Professional cricket is a hard school and no one does you any favours. Many other players had suffered the knocks, and at least I had pulled on the England sweater. The events of 1984 have helped me to enjoy my cricket more because I now react better to adversity.

A short trip to Zimbabwe in February 1985 helped me get out of my depression. Mike Vockins, the Secretary of Worcestershire, took out an English Counties side and we had a very enjoyable month on and off the field. The cricket was of a high standard, the social life good, and yours truly played well. It was good to be with a group of talented young players as well as the likes of Nick Cook, Paul Terry and Andy Lloyd who had shared the same fate as me: playing against the West Indies and missing out on the India tour. Life was going on for them, and their resilience bucked me up.

When I started the English season I was thinking too positively. My good form in Zimbabwe made me think I could play more assertively back in England. 'I'll show them,' I thought as I vowed that the public would not remember that awful Lord's Saturday for very long. I should have known better: with my limited strokeplay there was no mileage in trying to crash the ball all over the place against class bowlers over a hectic season. In the first few weeks, as I tried to play like a millionaire, I got out playing uncharacteristic shots. I was lofting the ball far too often while trying to compile big hundreds in attractive fashion. As a result I fell between two stools early on and that was no good for me or for my county. At last I came to my senses and reverted to my normal way of playing. It dawned on me that with Graham Gooch back in the fold there was no way that I would displace Tim Robinson as his partner, not least of all because Robbo started off the season so magnificently. His confidence was obviously very high after his excellent tour, and a superb 175 in the First Test at Leeds showed he had improved even more. He got another hundred in the series and we were all struggling to recall any other young batsman who had looked so composed and certain so early in his Test career. In 1984 he used to flirt a little outside the off stump, but throughout the 1985 season he knew exactly where his stumps were. He played superbly off front and back foot on both sides of the wicket and looked the complete opening batsman. I knew I had no chance of getting a look in with Robbo playing so well, so I concentrated on getting big scores in my own fashion on behalf of my county – then, who knows, I might get considered for the winter tour? After all, it was to the West Indies!

Clive Rice, the Nottinghamshire captain, is a great one for setting his players individual targets at the start of each season and he pins them up on the notice board in our dressing-room. Some of the lads disagree with the idea, but I approve of it; if a man like Richard Hadlee can push himself towards these goals, we should not be too proud. In April 1985 Clive asked me to get 1,600 runs in first-class games and

I did my very best: I made almost 1,800 and although I only got two centuries, I was pleased with that after snapping out of my early-season delusions of grandeur. I got a big hundred – 171 – against Derbyshire, even though they were convinced I was caught in the slips in my 40s. If I had thought the ball had carried to Bruce Roberts I would have been off like a shot, but when I stood my ground I was roundly abused by some of my opponents. When I got to my hundred they did not applaud but that did not bother me. When I believe I am out, I do not hang around waiting for the umpire's decision: I will not be hypocritical like those bowlers who complain about non-walkers then stand their ground when it is their turn to bat. In that Derbyshire match I was pleased at the way I concentrated through all the flak, and it felt as if I was running into form. A good hundred against Yorkshire got me some pleasing press coverage, especially when it was announced that I was on stand-by for the Old Trafford Test with Tim Robinson struggling with a back injury. I was not officially informed of that, and in any event Tim recovered to play, but it was nice to be easing myself back into contention again. I was well aware that a good August and September impresses the selectors much more than a good May when a touring party is being chosen, so I just kept on churning out the runs and hoping.

When we played Gloucestershire in the quarter-finals of the NatWest Trophy in early August it was an important match for the Club and for my personal ambitions. Of course I wanted to do well against my old county and I was particularly keen to impress against their opening bowlers, David Lawrence and Courtney Walsh, who had been getting a lot of publicity after bowling out sides on green wickets. I knew there would be a lot of media attention on this game and I wanted to remind people that, with the West Indies tour looming, I could still play fast bowling as well as anyone. It went better than I dared hope, with Robbo and I putting on 146 for the first wicket, and we beat them by eleven runs. My opening partner again played magnificently in the semi-final at Worcester to get us to the final at Lord's and the stage was set for a happier September for both the Club and myself. It was time we picked up a trophy after a few near-misses.

Well, we had yet another agonizing near-miss, yet another disappointment in the last over. This time it was down to the last ball, when we needed just two runs. A catch to mid-wicket meant we had lost – to Essex – by a single run. We could hardly believe it had happened to us again, but it must be said it was a fabulous game of cricket, played in a wonderful atmosphere, in superb weather, with so many fine individual contributions. I hope I shall never be too one-eyed to ignore the wider aspects while concentrating on the aims of the team, and I suppose the most important feature of the game was that more than 20,000 fans went home happy to have seen such a great match. We should always keep those points in mind while we bemoan our fates in the privacy of the dressing-room.

Right from the moment that our lady physio started changing alongside us that morning, it was no ordinary day. Sheila Ball was the first lady physio to be allowed inside the hallowed portals of the Lord's pavilion, and she had no qualms about stripping down to her bra and panties and getting into her tracksuit; she was just a couple of places along from me as I clambered into my jock-strap. The conflicting reactions from all the lads helped ease the tension, and that morning I was determined to enjoy the day, whatever the result. A full house at Lord's is very special and I felt that I would give of my best if I did not get too wrapped up in all the tension.

It was a belting wicket, the best type for a one-day final because it means plenty of runs and a chance of a tight finish without the game being ruined when the wicket is dampish early in the day. We did not really do ourselves justice in the field, apart from sterling work by Eddie Hemmings which surprised those who could see no further than his ample girth and under-estimated his pride in performance and strong throwing arm. I dropped Kenny McEwan before he had scored: he hit a low full toss on the bottom of the bat and it looped over my head, but I still got both hands to it as it came over my right shoulder and I felt I ought to have held it. Kenny went on to make a crucial 46 not out. With Graham Gooch making 91 and Brian Hardie 110, their total of 280 for 2 was a formidable one. It did not help that Kevin Cooper missed out on bowling his last three overs, for one of our most reliable seamers did not operate when the slog was on. Instead Kevin Saxelby was kept on and disappeared for 73 in his 12 overs, while Cooper went for 27 in 9.

Saxelby also played a central role in a most unfortunate incident. I was standing at mid-off, and twice in an over Saxelby had been sluggish down on the Tavern boundary at third man. Each time the batsmen had scampered two instead of being restricted to one and Clive Rice was rightly irritated. With one ball of the over left, Rice motioned Saxelby to change places with Kevin Cooper at deep fine leg. Saxelby refused to move. He had been moping around in the deep, brooding about his expensive bowling, but in such an important game every player has to give his all in the field. Saxelby is of farming stock and very much his own man, but such open dissent was unfortunate.

At the start of our innings I let the others worry about the Saxelby incident. It was too important for Tim and I to give us a good start, otherwise we had no chance. At tea we were 124 for 0, compared to 130 for 0 by Essex in the same number of overs. We were on course, with some powerful strikers of the ball still to come. After the break, I just could not get going again and it was just as well that Ian Pont ran me out.

It was now up to the stroke-players. They all did their bit in varying degrees, but the key dismissal was that of Richard Hadlee. He had reached 22 in no time at all and was looking very dangerous when he stepped back to try to hit one over extra cover and was bowled. Ian Pont, their most inexperienced bowler, had done the trick just as our great all-rounder was winning the game comfortably.

Derek Randall was still there, at the end of a marvellous season for him, but it was now a tall order. Duncan Martindale, playing his first one-day game, settled down astonishingly quickly and they started to pick up the impetus again. With just three overs left, we were still 37 short. Then Derek started to improvise, stepping back towards the leg side and placing the ball through the vacant areas on the off. We still had an outside chance if he stayed in, even though the light was fading fast. When the last over started we needed 18 to win: Taunton 1984 all over again! Derek Pringle went for 16 in the first five balls as Randall manipulated the ball brilliantly into the gaps. By now we could hardly stand the tension in the dressing-room. I wanted to watch the end from the balcony but the superstitious ones in the team told me not to move, to stay inside and watch the final ball on the television.

At the start of that final over, I thought it odd that there was no man out on the cover boundary, where Derek had been picking up so many runs. When he continued to cream the ball away in that direction I thought it even odder. I simply hoped that Keith Fletcher was not being extra wily, that he had forgotten to put a man out there. It just shows the fine dividing line between success and failure: if we had got two runs off that final ball, the best tactician in the county game would have been blamed for his field placing! Fletcher had one crucial role to play, though. After endless fidgeting and spitting on to the pitch from Randall, the bowler and fielders were ready. England bowler against England

batsman. *Just get a bat on it, Derek and run like hell!* Just as
Pringle started on his run-up, Fletcher told him to stop.
Second thoughts about the field setting. More consultations.
More twitching from poor Randall. Finally Pringle bowled
the final ball and Derek hit it straight to Paul Prichard at
mid-wicket, twenty-five yards away. 'Oh, no! Not again!
How can he hit it straight to a fielder?' we all shouted. It was
such a deflating moment: if he had just touched a bat on the
ball they would have run at least a single, then chanced it on
the throw, but a little scoop into the hands of mid-wicket . . .!
It would have been better to mishit the damned thing!

Derek Randall staggered into the dressing-room, hair
matted, sweat pouring off him, and he looked pathetic. I felt
so sorry for him: he had done so much to get us there. This
time there were no tears – a Championship is a good deal
more prestigious than winning a Lord's final – but a general
feeling that it had been a great day out and we had almost
won a famous victory, going for the highest total to triumph
in a one-day final. We all played the 'if only' game, though:
if only I had caught McEwan, if only Cooper had bowled all
his overs, if only Hadlee had not got himself out, if only
Derek had stood still for that final ball as it was speared
down the leg side. Ultimately one delivery was sent down in
hope to a batsman who could hardly see it in desperate light
and that decided the game.

A fortnight later I was pruning the roses at home in the
September sunshine, reflecting on a satisfactory personal
season and a frustrating one for my county. I was mulling
over my chances of being picked for two England tours: the
big one to the West Indies or the B trip to Zimbabwe,
Bangladesh and Sri Lanka. I was trying to be as dispassionate
as possible, but kept coming back to the feeling that I must
get a place on one of the trips. It was generally acknowledged
that my strong point was the way I dealt with fast bowling,

that I had not been overwhelmed by the West Indies in 1984, that my form had held up since then. I was not shell-shocked, I clearly relished the spice of physical danger and the high-wire act which facing the quicks involves. On the other hand I had been to Zimbabwe a few months earlier and had batted well, and that experience would surely be of relevance if they wanted to send me on the B tour. As I wondered when the tour parties would be announced, I happened to look through the lounge window and saw that Carole was crying. I came in by the back door, walked into the lounge, and she said, 'You're not in either side, how can they do this to you?' She was looking at 'Ceefax' on the television and slowly it dawned on me: it was September 1984 revisited.

David Smith was in the senior tour party. I could see the sense of that: a fine player of fast bowling, with a combative approach, there was no reason why he would not do a good job. I was very curious about the openers in the B squad, though: Kim Barnett, Wilf Slack and Martyn Moxon. No complaints about Slack – he had scored close to 2,000 runs in 1985 – but I had never regarded that fine stroke-player Kim Barnett as an opener, he never seemed tight enough to me. Moxon still had not played for England, and I had scored more runs than him in this last season. I found myself thinking, 'I was one of the top two batters in 1984. I improved my runs total this year, but now I'm not even in the top six for England. I'm probably not even in the top ten!' So much for an impressive showing in a one-day final in September. Due to the fact that I had no idea when the two squads were to be announced, I had not built myself up to the same peak of anticipation as the previous September, but the longer I thought about the composition of the parties, the more annoyed I felt. It hurt that I was not in contention, that my useful performances in difficult circumstances against the West Indies had seemingly been ignored. Would I ever get the chance to see if I could do myself justice at the highest level? It would not be for the want of trying: this winter, I would not mope around at Trent Bridge, listening to the news about Tim Robinson and Bruce French on the senior England tour. Good luck to them, they both deserved it – but if I did not get away I would not be in the right frame of mind for the next English season, one that was clearly going to be an important one for me.

After Carole dried her tears we both agreed that the priority was for us to go abroad for the winter in search of some good quality cricket. I would try my utmost to score a stack of runs and return to England to force the selectors to pick me. It was one of the best decisions we have made.

7

1986: The Wheel Comes Full Circle

I did not realize it at the time, but a new-born baby that weighed just over two pounds was a happy omen for my Test career. Carole gave birth to Stuart in June of 1986; he was eight weeks premature but the fantastic work of the staff at Nottingham City Hospital meant he was safe and well. As I watched him take his first vital gulps of oxygen, I thought of the last time I had become a father. Gemma was born in 1984, the last year I had played for my country. Would a second child change my luck and see me in the Test side before the end of 1986? The rest, as they say, is history.

I suppose I got back on the England scene for various reasons: good form in the summer, a lack of consistency from the openers tried by England, the absence of Graham Gooch from the Australian tour, and the feeling that the Australians would unearth a Thomson or a Hogg from nowhere to test those who did not face fast bowling with the same relish as myself. The fact that there was no bowler of genuine pace when we got to Australia did not bother me; I was determined to fill my boots and make it very hard for anyone to keep me out of the England team for a long time to come.

By the time I had returned to England in the spring of 1986 I was in a good frame of mind and set on making the coming season count. I would have been less than human if I had not noticed that Tim Robinson averaged just 9 in the Test series against the West Indies. Of course I felt sorry for him, but as a professional I saw it as a chance to get back in contention. It sounded as if he and the other batters had really suffered a mauling, and I knew that some of them would be shell-shocked for a time afterwards, especially as the new English season was hard on the heels of the Caribbean nightmare. I had no idea where I stood in the pecking order and the decision to send Wilf Slack from the B tour to replace the injured Mike Gatting in the West Indies had not exactly filled me full of optimism. After all, I was on the official stand-by list, along with Neal Radford and Dipak Patel and the B squad was already short of an opener with Kim Barnett back home with a virus. Clearly I had a lot to do to force my way back.

At least I had done something positive during the winter. Carole and I had agreed that I could not face any more sympathy from well-meaning acquaintances and while I was waiting to be fixed up abroad I took a short tour to Jamaica to play for an International Eleven against the West Indies. It was galling to think I might have been out there a few months later with England, but a consoling word from Roger Harper and Clive Lloyd was appreciated, and I enjoyed the 94 I scored on coconut matting against Marshall, Holding, Garner, Patterson and Walsh. By now I was not bitter about missing out on the tour, merely philosophical and determined to play well for whatever side sought my services that winter.

That side turned out to be Orange Free State in South Africa. I have Carole's shrewd business sense to thank for that. While I was in Jamaica she took a phone call from Ali Bacher, the prominent official of the South African Cricket

Union. He explained that Orange Free State needed someone to replace Alvin Kallicharran and Arnie Sidebottom who had both pulled out through injuries. Graeme Fowler and Paul Allott had been contacted but were committed elsewhere. They had been kind enough to recommend me, and after Bacher had phoned Clive Rice for a recommendation the call was put through to my home. Apparently Bacher was very impressed by Carole's businesslike negotiations and the deal was concluded while I was in Jamaica. She did a very good job: negotiations also brought me the captaincy of the side, an important stimulus. I wanted to get as much experience as possible of overseas cricket and captaining a first-class side was a bonus.

We had a terrific time in South Africa. It was always going to be a difficult year for the Free State as they faced their first season in the A section of the Currie Cup, but we had a marvellous team spirit in a young, keen side and, with luck, we might have won three of our six Currie Cup games. I played well – getting 88 and a century against Natal – and I enjoyed the duel with Graham Dilley who was opening the bowling for Natal. He was out there trying to regain full fitness and form after a series of worrying injuries, and with John Lever acting as Natal coach he did not lack excellent technical advice. He cut down his run-up, learned how to swing the ball late, and looked a high-class bowler. I came back thinking he was a certainty for England that summer and I was delighted to see him break through on the Australian tour.

I enjoyed the captaincy and the responsibility it brought. From a rather defensive outlook early on I changed for the better over the season, backed a few hunches and took a few chances. The young Free State team responded well to my desire for punctuality and smart dress, and if they thought I was an old-fashioned fuddy-duddy, no one said so. I happen to like to see first-class cricketers smartly turned out in blazers and ties, it shows a pride in one's profession. All in all, I felt I had put something into the future of Orange Free State cricket, and I looked forward to returning there the following winter in the absence of an England call.

For long periods of the 1986 season it seemed as if I would be heading back to South Africa. Graham Gooch had a plentiful supply of opening partners for England: Graeme Fowler, Tim Robinson, Wilf Slack, Mark Benson, Bill Athey, Martyn Moxon, plus Wayne Larkins, who was selected but pulled out through injury. No Chris Broad, though. Gooch is the outstanding English opener without a doubt and I have always had great admiration for the natural talent of Larkins, but I would be lying if I claimed not to believe myself to be as good as the others. Yet I had no idea what the selectors thought of me, because none of them had talked to me after the Sri Lanka Test back in 1984.

My confidence was high at the start of the English season, but for some reason I kept getting out in the Championship games, even though I could do no wrong in the limited-overs matches. Perhaps I was subconsciously in sympathy with my partner, Tim Robinson. He looked awful early on, a total contrast to his marvellous standard of 1985. Early in the season we put on 159 in the John Player League match against Hampshire but we both played tentatively as Malcolm Marshall beat the bat time and again. It was the same in our first Championship match of the season, when somehow we kept Marshall out to put on 76, but it was clear that we were not at our best. Tim appeared to have a problem with all black fast bowlers: he was drawing away to leg, leaving his off stump unguarded and looking anything but secure. To my annoyance I was picking up his insecurity.

For some reason all that changed after I had picked up the

ultimate ignominy – a 'pair'. It happened at Leicester at the end of June, when James Whitaker caught me at gully, then at backward short leg. It may seem strange but I was pleased that I had battled away for almost half an hour to try to avoid the dreaded second nought. I did not give way under the pressure and fear of failure; I eventually fended off an unplayable ball from Winston Benjamin and it went in the air. My mind went back to the only other time I had got a pair – for Gloucestershire Seconds – and I remembered that in the next game I went out and scored a hundred. I would aim for a repeat performance. There was no real reason why I was not getting runs in the Championship, other than a lack of concentration and the fact that in the limited-overs games the absence of close fielders meant I was under no pressure. It was about time I started to get runs in all competitions.

In the next Championship match history repeated itself. I scored a hundred against Warwickshire, then soon afterwards a good 122 against Yorkshire as Robbo and I added over 200. On the first day of that Warwickshire game the umpire Peter Wight unwittingly ignited the flame of England ambition in me. We were batting and he said to me, 'Guess who's been called in to replace Wayne Larkins in the Test?' I had no idea, could not even guess, and he said, 'Mark Benson.' I remember saying, 'Benson!' to him, and then wondering what was in the minds of the selectors. This is not meant unkindly, but I did believe I was a better player than the Kent opener. Then I realized he had forced his way through by scoring a lot of runs in the first two months of the season. I said to myself, 'Right, if Benson gets in, so can I. He's had a good two months, I'm going to have an even better two months from now on.' It really spurred me on and the runs flowed. Robbo and I put on 221 against Gloucestershire at Cheltenham (those lovely short boundaries!) and I was pleased at the way I played Walsh and Lawrence, a fact picked up by

the various national cricket writers. It never does any harm
to get runs against the team at the top of the table!

By this time, in mid-August, England still lacked a settled
opening partnership. The team had developed a siege men-
tality after the West Indian nightmare. The worst thing to
happen was losing the First Test against India, because it cost
David Gower the captaincy and Mike Gatting needed time
to bed down into the job, while everyone else was lacking in
confidence. With Ian Botham suspended there was no one of
stature to put the Indians or the New Zealanders in perspective. As a result Richard Hadlee was having a great time
against our batters. Martyn Moxon was dropped for the final
Test at the Oval and for the first time in my career I was glad
not to be picked as his replacement. I had no idea how I
would be able to cope with the mental demands of batting
against a great bowler who was also my county colleague.
Presumably Richard Hadlee knew exactly where to bowl at
me and he had the big-match experience to prosper at my
expense. If I had been recalled I would have been on a hiding
to nothing: I would have been awash with memories of my
last, appalling Test innings, and if Hadlee had rolled me over
that would have surely been my last chance wasted at the
highest level. Clive Rice thought I should have played at the
Oval. In the local press he said that the left-hand/right-hand
combination messes up Richard's line, and that he tends to
pitch a lot on middle and leg to the left-hander rather than
the danger area of around off stump. On any other occasion
I would have been flattered at my captain's recommendation,
but Richard is such a great professional that I was relieved not
to be asked to face him. For once I would have subconsciously
disobeyed my cardinal rule; I would have been aware who
was bowling at me. Now, I would have no worries about
batting against him in a Test match, because I have since
learned so much about the mental stresses and gained some

success. In August 1986 I would have been unable to do myself justice.

Throughout that summer people had said to me, 'This is a good time for you not to be in the England side,' and I could see what they meant. It was clear that the side was still shell-shocked and not performing to its true potential. All they needed was a win or two to get the media off their backs, but it was not to be and both India and New Zealand cashed in. Apart from the Oval Test, I really wanted to be out there, because I knew from bitter experience that you can quickly be placed in the 'out' tray. I was very keyed up to end the season with a series of big scores, because past experiences had taught me that the selectors do take notice of a late run. Three Championship centuries in September did me some good, and I was particularly pleased with the one against Sussex because Imran Khan charged in at me and really tested me out. He was the first to congratulate me after I scrambled a single to reach my hundred, and such a gesture from a great international bowler did my confidence no harm at all. Nor did a century against Essex on the opening day of the final Championship game when the top cricket writers were at Trent Bridge to report on another title for Essex.

That hundred against Essex was very much a celebratory one because twenty-four hours earlier I had achieved my ambition: I had been picked to go on the plum tour, with England to Australia. This time I was prepared for the radio announcement at ten o'clock and I was counting the minutes when the phone rang at home. It was the England captain, Mike Gatting, to congratulate me. In the emotion of the moment I blurted out, 'Is Robbo going as well?' to be told 'No, Slacky's got the vote.' My immediate reactions were selfish ones – it was the best tour of all, I was back in the frame, I was right never to have given up hope – and it was some time before I could spare any thoughts for Robbo. I listened to the radio news at ten o'clock, eleven o'clock and at midday to ensure I had not dreamed Gatting's phone call; after the disappointments of the two previous Septembers, it took some time to settle my emotions.

I thought of Carole and how soon I could tell her. She was in hospital having a minor operation and I knew she would still be out for the count. I could not talk to her until mid-afternoon and she told me how she found out: a kindly, cricket-mad surgeon had placed a note by her bedside, and when she woke up she read the message: 'Page the Oracle'. She switched on the television, flicked the appropriate code and there was the side with her husband included. It was all a bit hazy for her after the operation and she went straight back to sleep. A few hours later she woke up with a start and 'paged the Oracle' again to check she had not been dreaming. Suspension of belief was the common currency among the adults in the Broad household that day!

Next morning I reported for duty at Trent Bridge for the Essex match. When I walked into our dressing-room I felt warmly emotional as I was showered with sincere congratulations from my team-mates. By now I was wondering how Robbo and I would react to each other on our first meeting since the selection. I recalled how stiff it had been between us two years earlier when he got in ahead of me for India. A few minutes later he walked into the dressing-room and went straight to his usual changing area, which is well away from me. He did not talk to me, but I understood that. When I walked out to look at the wicket Graham Gooch was already out there and he was very warm in his congratulations; I joked with him that I only got picked for England when he was unavailable. Robbo was also out in the middle at that time, but again he said nothing to me about the tour party. When we batted on that first morning he looked very dispirited and lethargic, and gave the general impression that he wished the season was over.

I can appreciate his reticence with me. He is a proud individual, with high standards on and off the field and I was wondering if he had made the fatal error of being too publicly confident about his chances for the tour. I recalled a chat we had a fortnight earlier at Hove. Robbo had made a big undefeated hundred in the previous game against Kent at Trent Bridge, a match watched by the England selector Phil Sharpe. He clearly felt in good nick again, that he had timed his resurgence right for the final deliberations, because he mentioned the tour party to me while we were hosing down in the shower. 'Who would you take, then, now that Goochy's not going?' I asked and he replied, 'Moxon, Robinson and Broad.' Not a word about Bill Athey who had played in the final Test and scored a magnificent unbeaten hundred to win the one-day international at Old Trafford. I thought to myself, 'Steady on, Robbo, stranger things have happened. We might both miss out.' I spoke from bitter experience and felt that Robbo was being dangerously over-optimistic. Despite some good scores I felt he was nowhere near as solid as in 1984, and definitely not in the same league as his 1985 form. To me, he needed further rehabilitation, but I had given up trying to read the minds of the selectors. When my team-mates came up with their annual tour party they selected both Robbo and myself, and I had to remind them that they had also selected me in the two previous years! All sorts of other names were being bandied about: Ashley Metcalfe, Paul Terry, Wilf Slack, even young Andy Moles in his first season with Warwickshire. There was nothing to be gained from waiting and hoping, we should steel ourselves for disappointment.

Yet I would have been more upset at missing out in 1986 than in the two previous years because I was now playing better than ever. I had fallen short of Clive Rice's target of

1,600 Championship runs by just 7 and had made more than 2,000 in all competitions. I was hitting the ball better than ever and, within my limitations, playing very consistently. If I had missed out on that tour to Australia I would have been justified in packing the game up, or at least rationalizing the fact that I would never again get a chance at the highest level. I was a fortnight away from my twenty-ninth birthday and unlikely to get any better. It was now or never for me and, thank God, I got the chance. The memory of Tim Robinson's England gear came flooding back to me: it was 1984, I was brooding in the marketing department at Trent Bridge and Robbo's name was plastered all over equipment arriving from Lord's. I was envious that I was missing out on that lovely touring sweater and all those instructions from Lord's. Little things like that spur you on, you want to be part of the big-time, even down to the blazer and the cap. Now I had really arrived.

My selection seemed to be favourably received by the cricket scribes. A surname like mine always leads to awful puns among the headline-writers ('A Broad Hint' and all that imaginative stuff), but the writers seemed to accept I had earned another chance. John Woodcock, the cricket correspondent of *The Times*, had doubts about my ability to push the score along, and he wrote: 'I can't honestly say that I look forward with great relish to seeing Broad and Slack, two dourish left-handers, opening England's innings in Sydney; but they may still do a very fair job.' As for my fielding, Tony Lewis in the *Sunday Telegraph* wrote, 'Broad is a bit on the stiff side.' True I am no Colin Bland, but at the end of the tour I was delighted when my county colleague Bruce French told me how impressed he had been with my fielding. That was due to extra confidence because I was batting so well and the team was playing with so much gusto: we all felt we could afford to go for the half chance and not worry too much if we spilt it, because at least we had been positive.

I was perfectly happy for the press to assume I would play nothing but dour innings. They were entitled to their opinion, but I just felt very pleased with my prospects. It was with shoolboyish glee that I opened all the various bits of correspondence about the tour from headquarters. Having heard so much about how team spirit is always so much better on tour, I could not wait to get to know all the lads, to experience everything for the first time. Some may have felt it was my last chance to prove myself, but for me it was the first chance.

8

The Tour of a Lifetime

By the end of England's tour to Australia Mike Gatting was calling me 'Whoda' – as in 'Whoda thought it of you, Broady?!' Who indeed? The combined achievements of the team and myself were beyond the realm of fantasy. Within a few months we had routed the cynics and I had returned laden with awards and, at least statistically, in very impressive company. In the last few weeks of the tour we were getting a tremendous amount of mail from well-wishers and genuine cricket fans back home and we were all so proud that we had given them something to shout about as the snowdrifts piled up.

Sheer novelty made me decide to keep a daily diary of the four-and-a-half months in Australia. It was to be my first England tour and I was determined to lodge it all in the memory bank. As I flick through the pages of my diary I can recall many golden moments, an occasional low day, but an abiding sense of personal and team satisfaction. The team that had been derided throughout the English summer and lampooned in the first weeks of the Australian tour had become the first to win all three competitions in the space of just a few weeks. Carole and Gemma came out to boost personal morale, whilst Stuart was cared for by Carole's parents back home in England.

I sensed it was to be no ordinary tour on the first evening when we all gathered at the hotel at Heathrow Airport. In the bar Graham Dilley introduced me to a quiet chap, dressed all in black, called Eric. We shook hands and I thought no more of it. When I saw him talking to old hands like Ian Botham, David Gower and Allan Lamb, I asked Dilley who he was. 'Don't you know?' 'Of course not, why do you think I'm asking?' 'That's Eric Clapton.' *The* Eric Clapton, one of the rock world's greatest legends. To people of my age-group he was a huge name. Little did I know that within a few weeks I would be chatting away to other mega-stars like Elton John and Phil Collins. I was unaware that rock stars are as keen about sport as we cricketers are about their music: both strands of the entertainment business would be happily entwined on the tour.

Before we managed to relax in the company of Messrs John and Collins we had experienced the ups and downs of touring in a big way. Nobody in our party would admit it at the time but we started badly and we deserved the stick we got from the media. In the first month the experienced players did not pull their weight, adopting a languid air as if to say, 'It's going to be a long tour, there's no point in getting carried away by working too hard too soon.' In the end they were right – they had the practical knowledge to pace themselves – but we newcomers and younger players lacked direction early on. We found ourselves dragged down to the level of treating each match like a benefit game. Micky Stewart, our cricket manager, kept the media at bay by shouting at the younger players in the nets and generally giving an air of bristling command, but we were not the real problem in those early weeks. David Gower was a particular worry. He had had an awful year, losing the captaincy of both England and Leicestershire on top of his mother's death, and in those early weeks he looked listless and peripheral. So David opted to coast along before the First Test and the management had a problem. I remember one morning in Perth, before the first Test, when the media were singing a derisive chorus about our prospects. While the rest of us loosened up on the outfield, Micky Stewart was closeted in the dressing-room having a quiet word with Lamb, Botham and Gower. I have no idea what was said, but they certainly looked interested shortly afterwards when we came to Brisbane and the serious action.

Yet a week before the Brisbane Test we still looked awful. On the first day against Western Australia we dropped seven catches, and then got dismissed for 152 on a perfect wicket. We scraped a draw, but my diary records this verdict on the press criticism: 'If the truth be known they are, in the main, right. It always hurts to know the truth.' Our experienced tourists would laugh it off, saying, 'You know what the press are like, they love to knock us,' but they had enough justification in that first month. The Aussies were favourites to win the series after showing a lot of resilience in India, whereas in this first month our batsmen had looked strangely vulnerable to a clutch of left-arm fast-medium bowlers operating over the wicket. Perhaps it was the different light or the extra bounce in the wickets, but collectively our batting was unimpressive. I had played in every game and had made just one 50 in three first-class games while choosing all sorts of daft ways to get myself out. Luckily for me, Bill Athey and Wilf Slack were struggling and I looked the best of the three possible openers: poor Slacky in particular was grappling with his form in the nets whereas I seemed to be playing securely. If they had exerted more pressure on me by scoring heavily I might not have got into the Test side.

By the time we got to Brisbane for the opening Test it was

clear that we had to go up a few gears. Getting to Brisbane three days before the game was a good move: it gave us time to settle in, get used to the conditions and prepare mentally. On the eve of the Test we had a very constructive team dinner. Mike Gatting and Micky Stewart left us in no doubt that we had to perform ten times better than in the first month, that the time for excuses was over. The point was hammered home that it was vital not to lose the First Test, because the Australians were very confident and we must not boost them any further. Ian Botham weighed in with some constructive, positive thoughts: he said Australian Tests were the big ones, and that he hoped nobody would offer his wicket up by walking before the appeal was given. That was significant – Botham always 'walks' in England if he knows he has nicked it. It was good to see that our great all-rounder was so pumped up to get at the Aussies.

The atmosphere on the first morning really got to me. I loved it – the traffic jams around the Gabba, the long queues for tickets, the throngs of spectators around our nets. It was just like Lord's 1984 all over again, except it was hotter. I found it all very inspirational. A big crowd always inspires me and, with the Gabba one of the smallest Test arenas in Australia, the atmosphere was intimate and tingling. It was the big-occasion feeling that every international sportsman relishes, and I really wanted to fight it out for England on that first morning. I gritted my teeth and concentrated harder than at any other time on the tour. The overcast, humid conditions favoured the bowlers but I think they were affected by the tension and at no stage did they put the ball in the right area. Bill Athey and I were able to leave a lot, and although I was out after forty-five minutes we established a psychological advantage, because they knew they ought to have made us play at a lot more deliveries. I was annoyed at getting out, although it was a good delivery from Bruce Reid which pitched just outside off stump as I was committed to the stroke. I got a faint edge but stood there, mindful of Ian Botham's words at the team dinner. Nobody had disagreed with Botham, and throughout the series we waited for the umpire to make the decision. This time Tony Crafter was right and I had to go.

We did well to finish that first day on 198 for 2. Mike Gatting had replaced me and the decision was thoroughly vindicated. With Gower so much out of form, we needed a positive response at number three and the captain was the ideal man. Bill Athey held firm all day as the pressure visibly eased. They had not cashed in before lunch and, as the ball lost its hardness and shine, we batted very professionally. Two more good sessions next day and we were almost certain to avoid defeat, which was always the first priority.

One of the most significant days of the entire series saw David Gower achieve some semblance of form and Ian Botham bludgeon a typical hundred. Gower was dropped in the slips before he scored and for a long time looked unrecognizable. Slowly he groped his way to a half-century that, by his own standards, was mediocre, but at least he had spent some time out in the middle, coming to terms with his footwork and the bowling. In the second innings, he was to play far better and in the next Test he scored a glittering, princely hundred. For his part Botham re-established the hex that he has exerted over the Aussies since his amazing deeds in 1981. Everything was geared up for him this day. We had lost two quick wickets and unless he stayed in and played properly we could be dismissed for around 300. He had just signed a three-year contract to play for Queensland and he clearly wanted to impress his new employers. Above all it was England *v*. Australia; his attitude was unrecognizable from that of the last time I had been with him in an England dressing-room. Gone was the bored, crabby team-mate of

1984; instead he was tremendously supportive, continually positive and resolutely determined to come out on top. When you graft such attributes on to his great natural talents you have a wonderful cricketer and invaluable team-mate.

It was the kind of innings that the professionals do not want to miss, when you resent going to the toilet in case you miss anything. For me only Martin Crowe, Richard Hadlee and Viv Richards have a similar aura. Botham played himself in carefully, taking advantage of the short boundaries on this compact ground. Allan Border tried to frustrate him by just giving him singles, but he placed the ball masterfully into the vacant areas. At lunch he was 80-odd not out and after taking his gear off he sat there, smoking a small cigar, saying very little. It was not the extrovert Botham that the public see; he was determined to make everything count. He was just biding his time, and when they took the new ball he climbed into Merv Hughes and hit him all over the place. Derek Stirling had suffered in the same way in Botham's last Test innings at the Oval, and here we had another inexperienced bowler, trying his heart out, but unable to locate anything other than the middle of Botham's bat. Even to hardened English pros, it was wonderful. He had done it again and he even took time out to encourage Phillip DeFreitas in a highly promising first Test innings. He had taken DeFreitas under his wing in those early weeks – a shrewd management move to have them rooming together – and it was good to see Botham coaxing him along.

Before the day ended the Australians had lost their first wicket through a good piece of captaincy by Mike Gatting. He moved me round to wide-ish mid-on and the very next ball I caught David Boon there from a long hop by DeFreitas. I have no idea what Gatting was thinking about, but it certainly looked good. Everything seemed to be going our way: Botham had again established a significant dominance,

Gower had spent valuable time in the middle, DeFreitas looked as if he had been playing Test cricket for years, and we had ensured we would not lose. On top of all that we had just one more day to see if we could make them follow on, then a rest day would give us time to recharge the batteries and go for victory. It worked perfectly, and they failed to avoid the follow on by 9 runs. Graham Dilley at last broke through his own psychological barrier by taking five wickets in a Test innings for the first time, and my mind went back to the previous winter when he had been so impressive in South Africa. Before his injuries he had simply run in and tried to knock the batsman's head off: now that he lacked the mental confidence to bowl at his fastest, so he just had to develop swing. He thought more about his bowling, even developed a slower delivery, stopped thinking about being England's shock bowler, and concentrated on being our best bowler. Time and again on this tour he produced the great delivery that leaves the batsman late and takes an edge.

So we had two days to take 10 wickets, and although we had to work hard on the fourth day we wrapped it up just after lunch on the final day. They panicked against John Emburey's nagging accuracy and we only needed 75 to win. To my great delight, I made the winning stroke – off the back foot through the covers off Merv Hughes – and we were home after exceeding our expectations. The Aussies were very sporting about it, although Allan Border was very dejected, blaming the press for talking down the England boys and letting the public think the home side were going to stroll to victory. That seemed a little rich: you cannot say the press know nothing about the game, then blame them for letting everyone think we were a pushover. I suspect Border was more concerned at the manner in which his team had folded on a good batting wicket, and also the havoc that Ian Botham might wreak before the series ended.

We left Border to his post-mortems and settled down to an excellent round of celebrations. That morning I had said to David Gower, 'If we win early, how long will the celebrations last?' and he replied, 'As long as possible.' We did not need to leave for the airport until midday the following day, so the champagne flowed and a great time was had by all. It was the first of several memorable parties, but I hasten to add they were all held at the right time – after hard work, with plenty of recovery time before the next game. That afternoon in Brisbane was an immensely satisfying one for us: we had been written off by many good judges and we could not really blame them. Luckily it was 'alright on the night', and our experienced players had pulled us out of the fire. I was pleased for Botham and company, because they had taken a lot of flak in the past year (some of it well deserved), but they had put the performance in when it was most needed. I was delighted for Mike Gatting, for having the sense to go in first wicket down and lead from the front. All things considered, Brisbane could not have gone any better and I do not think the Aussies really recovered from that mauling. Punctured hopes can deflate cricketers, especially when the optimism is excessive.

A week later we found ourselves in Perth for the Second Test, confident of going two up in the series. We named an unchanged side, but the Aussies dropped Merv Hughes and brought in Geoff Lawson. It was the first of many selection errors by them, because Lawson was not fully fit; at least Merv would have kept going at Perth, even though the wicket proved to be the kind I would want to carry around for the rest of my career. Before the Test there were several omens of varying nature. My parents flew in for a month's holiday and I dearly hoped I could score my first Test hundred for them. Yet the way I batted in the nets suggested I would be lucky to get off the mark: I hardly hit a ball in the middle of the bat on a wicket that was green and bouncy. As the ball seamed around, beating my bat regularly, I wondered if I was about to be found out at the highest level. I was so awful that I did not go near the nets again before the match in case my confidence was destroyed. A happier omen came at the Royal Perth Golf Club where I played the best round of my life in the company of Peter Lush, Mike Gatting and John Emburey – shrewd of me to keep in with the management! I remember hoping I would strike a cricket ball equally sweetly the next day. My prayers were answered on the most important day of my Test career so far.

I cannot believe I shall ever play as well again as I did on that first day when I finished 146 not out. I struck the ball so sweetly: two shots off the back foot through extra cover off Chris Matthews will linger in my memory for long time. Everything went right for us: Gatting won the toss, we batted first on an absolute belter of a pitch and the Aussies bowled badly at Bill Athey and myself. Lawson was clearly not fit, Chris Matthews could not put the ball in the right place and, by the time Bruce Reid came on as first change, our timing was working well and the ball was rapidly losing its shine. Bill and I could leave far too many deliveries early on, and it struck me that the bowlers were more nervous than the batters. We consolidated in the morning and just upped the tempo after that. Our main worry was the heat. Just before lunch it became terribly humid and I was worried about lasting out the whole day. A cold shower and the appearance of the Freemantle Doctor helped cool me down and we returned to the blissful prospects of grinding out a massive score against demoralized bowlers on the flattest pitch of all time. I wish batting was always as simple as that!

I gave a half chance to Lawson just after I reached 50, but

he was off-balance as he followed through. Bill was dropped before lunch in the slips by Allan Border off Chris Matthews, but after that – except for a few frenzied appeals that lacked any substance – it was plain sailing. At tea I was 98 not out. I had lost the strike in the previous over but I was surprisingly calm about the imminence of my first Test hundred. There was too much to do in the twenty minute interval to be all that nervous: cold shower, change into fresh gear, a quick bite of a sandwich and out again. In the first over after the break, Greg Matthews bowled me the ideal delivery and I was there. In retrospect I would have been furious to have missed out in such perfect batting conditions, but I was too elated to be so realistic at that moment. After that the priority was to get Bill to his century; Dean Jones had dropped him at square leg and he was looking more and more shaky as fatigue set in. At the end of each over I was down his end, saying, 'Come on, Bill, concentrate. Stay there and you've got it.' It was such a shame that he missed out by just four runs. Bruce Reid was praised for bowling him with an inswinging yorker, but in all honesty it was hardly a great delivery. Bill got himself out by playing the shot too early: he was there before the ball arrived, and in the end he toppled over while the ball squeezed through bat and pad. I felt very disappointed for him: when you add 223 for the first wicket in a Test match you want your partner to get a century as well, and he deserved one for his calmness.

Bill had played very well in the Brisbane Test in more exacting circumstances, and yet he felt he was still under pressure for his place. He had looked at our middle order and clearly came to the conclusion that he would not force his way into the Test side there, so he concentrated on the opening position. After his fine knock at Brisbane he would have been expected to keep his place for at least two Tests, even if he did not make a run, but an outburst by him between the first two Tests underlined the pressure he was feeling. We were playing at Newcastle against New South Wales and batting poorly on a slow wet wicket. Some of our batsmen did not fancy their regular positions in the order and Bill said: 'If one gets to drop down the order as a one-off, the same should apply to the rest of us. I'm not an opener: I never will be, but you're asking me to do the job.' That struck me as a very strange thing to say. After all he was part of a team that had just won the first Test, in which he had opened and played superbly. I put it down to the fact that Bill is a Yorkshireman. He is very dedicated and, although he will never admit it, he is like Geoffrey Boycott in the intensity of his professional approach to the job. Bill would never do a Derek Randall and agree to being shunted up and down the England batting order. He is very much his own man and is not a great communicator during a partnership. I like to have a chat with my partner at the end of an over, especially if there is something technical or encouraging to offer, but Bill would prefer to withdraw into his own thoughts and leave it to you to keep your spirits up. On the way out to bat we would talk and wish each other luck, but very little would pass between us after that. I suppose we are products of our different environments. Up in Yorkshire the game is taken very seriously and to an extent it can be a passport to a higher standard of living, whereas someone like me who came from a comfortable background and enjoyed the social side of the game would be a complete contrast. If I could step into a time machine, I am sure I would have loved playing as an amateur in the carefree days of striped blazers, country house matches and gaily coloured parasols. Money has never been a consideration to me in my cricket career: I am more keen on developing friendships and doing myself justice without compromising my personality. Bill Athey is much more single-minded and insular when batting, yet for all our temperamental differences we were becoming a useful opening pair.

I wish I could have transferred four of my runs to Bill's score on that first evening, but that was my only regret from a memorable day. At 272 for 2 we were again immune from defeat, although we knew that on such a flat wicket a lot of hard work lay in store. I was exhilarated as I was ushered from interview to interview, and I was overwhelmed by the warm reaction from men like Gower, Gatting and Botham, who had been down this particular road many times. I was not even tired, because I had hit so many boundaries that there had been few singles to scamper. Back in the hotel room I found a bottle of champagne from Wendy, my sister, and her husband, Tony, and another from Ian and Kath Botham, a typically kind gesture. The generous, unselfish side of Ian Botham's nature is something that his detractors ought to recognize.

Not surprisingly I slept very poorly that night. I played every shot over and over in my mind, and I was far too excited to settle. I even set myself a target: to beat Derek Randall's 174 against the Australians at Melbourne, and Tim Robinson's 175 in the Leeds Test of 1985. Somehow that seemed more important than topping my career best of 171. It was not to be. I never got going on the second morning. It seemed bizarre to raise my bat and acknowledge the crowd's applause after snicking a boundary through the slips off Lawson. As far as I was concerned I was now 4 not out, but David Gower disagreed. As I stood there, looking abashed as I raised my bat, he came down the pitch and said, 'Well done, great knock.' I said, 'Bloody awful shot, though,' only to be told, 'Listen you're 150 not out in a Test match – in a Test match. It doesn't matter how you got them, but you got them. Now go on and get some more.' Of course he was right, but I had played so well the day before that I wanted to carry on in the same vein. A limited stroke-player like me is bound to remember the days when it all clicked into place, whereas someone like Gower or Botham gets used to those inspirational occasions.

Soon I was caught behind off Reid as I played at a ball around off stump that I would have left alone at the start of my innings. I had only added 16 that morning and it was a bit of an anti-climax, but only because of the standard I had set the day before. Soon David Gower was to show me how a left-hander should bat. He hit a beautiful century that left us rapt in admiration for his gift of timing, his daring and his grace of execution. Over the years we had become accustomed to Gower's brilliance, but the innings by Jack Richards was the big surprise. It is true everything was set up for him – a flat wicket, tired bowlers, an old ball, a confident partner – but he really climbed into them. I had not seen a great deal of Jack's batting in county cricket, but I knew him to be a dedicated practiser and he did not look this gift horse in the mouth. He was full of confidence because he was keeping wicket well and that was reflected in his batting. After his Perth century, his glovework maintained its high standard, apart from a few lapses in the Sydney Test. Jack's success confirmed the importance of confidence and the need to be lucky – if our batters had shown better form in the run-in to Brisbane we might have gone in with Bruce French keeping wicket, but Jack was needed as insurance against yet another batting collapse. All credit to Jack: he seized his chance and did not let go.

After Jack passed his hundred we were pinching ourselves: could this possibly get any better? We were scoring so rapidly that we would have more than three days to bowl them out twice. It got even better when we dismissed David Boon on the second evening. With one day to come before the rest day, it was all falling beautifully into place. Test cricket was beginning to appear a very enjoyable exercise.

The rest of the game was much harder work. The wicket remained a good one, despite cracks that got wider and wider as the match progressed. The priority for Australia was to avoid the follow-on, and when Allan Border accomplished this his leap of delight indicated how much the opposition had lowered its sights since those heady pre-Brisbane days. Perhaps we got rather too negative as the game went on, but there was no point in giving them any elbow-room. I was delighted to pick up the Man-of-the-Match award and I assume my fielding tipped the balance ahead of the other high scorers. That may sound odd to those who have often seen me turn ones into twos in the outfield, but the extra confidence I gained from my batting was now there in my fielding – how else could I explain running out Dean Jones with a direct hit and taking a reflex catch at leg gully to get rid of Geoff Marsh?

Already, after just one Test hundred, I was being introduced to the perks of being a so-called celebrity. On this trip to Perth I met Elton John for the first time, after Ian Botham had arranged for tickets to see his concert. Dennis Lillee, Rod Marsh and Bruce Laird joined us backstage to have a drink with Elton before he performed, and it was an eye-opener. Elton was wearing a pink lion's mane that went halfway down his back, and a silver sequinned outfit with matching scarf and boots. He looked unbelievable, yet he seemed such a nice ordinary bloke who clearly loved sport. The concert was tremendous, and when I thanked him afterwards for the ticket he said, 'Thanks very much, Chris I'm glad you enjoyed it.' I was amazed that someone of his stature should remember the name of an insignificant cricketer. I had always loved Elton John's music, had bought almost every one of his albums, and it was a big enough thrill actually to meet him, never mind having him remember who I was. There were to be many more occasions on that tour when I would meet up with him and be touched by his love of cricket and his kindness, like the time in Adelaide when Carole had returned home and I was at a bit of a loose end until he invited me up to his suite for a meal and natter. By the end of the tour he was our unofficial seventeenth player in the tour party, and we were all knocked out by his genuine pleasure at our success and his generosity.

I met another musical hero in Perth at the same time as Elton John. Phil Collins was dining at the White Crusader Club in Freemantle when we rolled up with Ian Botham in typically extravagant Botham fashion. Kath Botham, Phillip DeFreitas, Graeme Fowler (out there coaching in Perth) and myself accompanied Both in a hired silver limousine: chauffeur, fridge, massive seats, right up his street. Ian leant forward, opened up the fridge, pulled out the inevitable bottle of champers and said, 'Go on Broady, crack it open,' so we arrived at the club in some style. When our hero spotted Phil Collins, they greeted each other like long-lost brothers and we were soon eating at the same table. Botham had certainly gone up the social ladder since he was a young tearaway at Taunton, happy with a glass of cider!

It was soon pretty clear that Elton John and Phil Collins were as interested in our side of the entertainment business as we were in their more glamorous world. Elton always wanted to know about the game's finer points, what we were trying to do out on the field and how you could combat specific bowlers. During the Adelaide Test he phoned me two nights in a row around midnight, just for a general chat about the day's play. The conversation on the second evening was a good deal more bizarre. The phone rang in my hotel room and it was Elton's publicist, Patti Mostyn, on the other end. 'Hello, Chris, I have the artiste here to speak to you' – Elton's nickname among his close associates, I later learned. We had another pleasant chat and after about twenty minutes the phone was returned to Patti who said, 'Aren't you a lucky boy, then, getting to talk to all these superstars?' I was completely thrown by that until she said I had been speaking to Phil Collins for half the time. It seemed Phil was on another line and just carried on the chat, without telling me that he had taken over from Elton. Admittedly their London accents are fairly similar, but I was floored by the way the hand-over had been so smoothly effected. I could not hear, never mind see the join! Phil came back on the line to confirm Patti's words and he wished a flabbergasted cricketer goodnight. This was proving to be a memorable first tour in more ways than one!

Between the Perth and Adelaide Tests we had the first – and only – smell of a scandal story involving one of the players. I had heard about the muck-raking that went on during recent tours and we were all very aware of our social responsibilities. To our delight there was nothing the sensation-seekers could latch on to, apart from the time when Mike Gatting overslept at Melbourne. Even then, no amount of digging and stirring could hype that story up, because it was a genuine fact. Mike Gatting simply overslept – it was nothing to do with women, drugs, booze or anything else. I know because I was the one who tried to wake him up and finally succeeded in getting a bleary-eyed captain out of bed and down to the Melbourne Cricket Ground.

We were due to play Victoria and I was looking forward to the game because it was the first one in which I was not playing. I was out on the ground an hour before the start, having a gentle loosener, when I spotted that the captain was nowhere to be seen. At 10.15 I mentioned this to Micky Stewart who said, 'Yes, it's funny, I rang this morning to his room and there was no reply.' What Micky did not know was that the dialling-out tone is similar to the engaged tone on Australian phones and that Gatt had failed to replace the receiver properly after phoning home the night before. By 10.20 I was wondering if I would have to play, because the sides have to be named half an hour before the eleven o'clock start. I was told to go back to the hotel a mile away and see if I could find Gatt. From the hotel lobby I encountered the same engaged tone on his room phone. When I banged on his door I finally got a very sleepy response and, after I shouted that he was due to play in half an hour, a volley of curses. He opened the door, looked very embarrassed and sleepy, and I helped him pack his gear in a hurry. As he shaved, I waited downstairs for him in the lobby. By now some of the straggling press men were going out to the ground, and somehow they found out.

By the time I drove the captain into the MCG, he was about twenty minutes late. The management had decided to say that he had suffered a bad attack of the trots but had now fully recovered. Trust Gatt to blow the cover, as he walked on to the field he adopted a gait that was a cross between a pregnant koala bear and a pigeon with dysentery! He played up to the official line and that simply mocked the story that had been fed to the press. Eventually Peter Lush had to tell the full story to the newshounds, which must have sounded suspicious after the earlier statement, but every word of the second statement was true. Later Phil Edmonds enjoyed some mileage out of the incident. Peter Lush had said that Gatt had apologized to the rest of the lads, but Phil pointed out at a team meeting that he was still waiting for his apology. Gatt had to stand up, looking very sheepish, and offer an apology, much to our hilarity. It was funny, despite the fact that he was in the wrong. Gatt is a very heavy sleeper and he was simply unaware that the phone was off the hook. Human error; end of story.

There were a couple of funny sequels to the Rip van Gatting incident. A few days later, as we flew from Melbourne to Adelaide, a stewardess came on the intercom and asked everyone on board to keep very quiet because Mr Gatting was asleep and must not be woken! Then a fortnight later, as we linked up with Noel Edmonds on a live television programme, Gatt was presented with an alarm clock! I must say he took the leg-pulling very well, especially as it lasted for several weeks. I am sure that some of the less scrupulous reporters who were out there just to manufacture some sleazy story must have been disappointed, but it was really just a storm in a pillow.

My diary entry for Sunday 14 December contains a typically English piece of understatement: '116, not a bad day.' Not a bad day, indeed: it was my second hundred in successive Tests against Australia. We had moved on to Adelaide, to another flat wicket with the short square boundaries beloved of B. C. Broad. Bill Athey and I had gone in to bat for the last half-hour on the second day after the Aussies had piled up more than five hundred. Our task was to avoid the follow-on and that would then kill the game stone dead. I really enjoyed that final half-hour on the Saturday night: I love the challenge of the fast bowlers roaring in and the fielders breathing down our necks. People tend to forget that in such circumstances the bowlers get nervous because they are expected to break through. With so many men round the bat there are lots of gaps, and if you get the ball through the inner cordon there is a good chance of a boundary. The same thing happened at Melbourne when they sprayed it around as they desperately sought a breakthrough.

My Adelaide hundred was nowhere near as fluent as the Perth one. The ball turned a fair bit for Peter Sleep and Greg Matthews and I had to graft a great deal. There are very few shots that reach the straight boundaries at Adelaide, so I had to run a good deal more than at Perth because a lot of my runs come straight in the 'V' between extra cover and mid-wicket. As a result I was shattered after this century. Without Mike Gatting's positive response I might not have got there. He really messed up the Aussie spinners, with the result that they would sometimes forget to bring in the field when I was on strike and I could play them easily away into the gaps, keeping the scoreboard ticking over and giving the more punishing batsman the strike. Sleep in particular was so demoralized by Gatting that he dropped short too often and I managed to get the square cut working quite well. I even managed my one and only six of the tour when I lapped Greg Matthews over the square leg boundary; as it soared away into the crowd I felt a pang of envy for the way Botham and Gatting manage that so often! Yet I was perfectly happy to play my own way and my hundred arrived through a stroke past extra cover to the boundary off Merv Hughes. My mind went back to a chat that morning with Peter West over breakfast. 'Nice to see another hundred up against the name of Broad,' he said. I agreed, fully aware that a lot of hard work lay ahead if that were to happen.

It was a pity that Bill Athey did not go on to a hundred at Adelaide. For the third Test in a row he played very well, got past his half-century, and then got out. He was furious at the way he got out – chopping a ball on to his stumps – and that Peter Sleep was the bowler. Sleep had got to Bill with all his histrionics on the field, and as Bill walked from the wicket he was beside himself with anger, raising his bat over his shoulder as if he could wrap it round the bowler's neck. Sleep had got on my nerves as well, acting like an Aussie from the Ian Chappell era, bawling at the batsman and appealing for everything. At one stage in this innings, after I had played a poor shot, Sleep ran down the pitch and screamed, 'You can't play, you're a f ... idiot.' I just laughed, and in the bar afterwards he came up and apologized. Nothing he could say would change my opinion of him and I agreed with Bill: there was no call to abuse me personally, as distinct from cursing his luck in frustration.

Sleep was the only Australian player who was objectionable on the field during the series. I was surprised at that. Before the tour began I had a word with John Edrich, a man who had suffered enough at the hands of the foul-mouthed Aussie players and spectators a decade earlier. He said the best way to deal with them is to stay out in the middle and score lots of runs. They would then at least respect you. If you tried to be pally with the crowd or the players they would tell you where to get off in no uncertain manner. It was good advice, but I was gratified at the good relationship between the two sides. Of course there were some flashpoints, some of which were misunderstood by the media, but there was very little 'sledging' on the field. Phil Edmonds, as you would imagine, gave out some choice words and he got them back with interest from the likes of Tim Zoehrer, but the rest of us found their rivalry rather funny, especially when they kept sending scurrilous poems about each other through to the dressing-rooms during the Melbourne Test. Phil would include some caustic remark about Zoehrer's wicket-keeping, while Tim would point up Phil's lack of hair and the fact that he was the insignificant husband of the famous Frances. Tim Zoehrer did not bother us on the field: we would laugh at his histrionics as he tried to cover up his inadequacies behind the stumps with a load of bluster. He bothered Greg Matthews far more than us: time and again Greg would wander away, muttering about Zoehrer's efforts. Greg thought that his New South Wales colleague Greg Dyer should be playing and he used to give Zoehrer some terrible volleys. I really liked Greg Matthews. A super chap, a genuine sportsman, he tried his hardest for his country. I know that many television close-ups gave the wrong impression, that he was slagging our batsmen off, but in reality he was cursing his own players because he felt they were not giving enough to the cause. The problem for the Aussies was that the captain Allan Border and his deputy David Boon were both quiet blokes and they said hardly anything on the field. So it was left to Greg Matthews and Dean Jones to do the geeing up on the field whereas all eleven of us would do that when we went out there.

Apart from Sleep's sledging at Adelaide, I only received one piece of flak on the field, and it also came during the Adelaide Test. I had given an interview in Perth after my hundred in which I pointed out that the Australians were struggling because so many of their best bowlers were playing in South Africa. A fairly reasonable statement, I thought, and a genuine attempt to play down my century and put it in perspective. By the time we got to Adelaide the inaptly named *Melbourne Truth* had distorted my remarks, and Merv Hughes was quoted, bristling fire and fury, predicting that he was going to knock my block off. Sure enough he got a bouncer to rifle past my nose early on in my Adelaide innings and I had to take swift evasive action. As I recovered my poise Greg Ritchie shouted from mid-off, 'How does that compare with your f ... rebels in South Africa, then?' I just laughed and looked away to recover my concentration. When I reached my century I stared hard at him as he applauded. In the dressing-room afterwards he told me that Allan Border had told him off because that remark seemed to spur me on. That was untrue, but it was an extra ingredient in making me concentrate fiercely.

So we managed to save the Adelaide Test comfortably enough, thanks to our solid reply, and some tight bowling by our spinners that meant the Australians could not score quickly enough to get among us with enough time to spare. It was a holding operation for us; with Ian Botham out with a rib injury we were down to four front-line bowlers and we knew we were highly unlikely to win the match. We felt we were much the better team, but the priority was to avoid defeat and hope the great man would be fit for the Melbourne Test.

Botham played at Melbourne, although not fully fit. Yet Ian Botham at 60 per cent is better than the rest of us at full power, especially against the Australians. They seemed to shrink in confidence when they knew he was going to play. Operating off a shortened run, he conned many of them out on the first day. He just turned his arm over on a greenish wicket and used his brains, picking up five wickets through a series of ambitious shots. Somehow Botham gets Australians into a self-destructive frame of mind and they do not treat him like an ordinary bowler: they play awful shots at him and he just cleans up, grinning all over his face. I am convinced that 1981 still lingered in the minds of many of the Australian players: they fully expected him to work wonders at any stage. One of Botham's main strengths as a bowler is that he is also a batsman; he understands the psychology of batting, he can recognize if the batter is twitchy or if he is shaping to play a particular shot. Botham is a master of different bouncers: first the slow lollipop, then the quicker one that gets you top-edging the hook. Throughout our team discussions he was always interesting about where to bowl at the Aussies, who had weak points, and who did not fancy the short-pitched delivery.

If the Aussies got themselves out to Botham, it was partly due to Gladstone Small's nagging accuracy and tireless example at the other end. Gladstone was an inspirational selection once Graham Dilley had been ruled out with a sore shoulder. The Australians kept selecting the wrong eleven, yet everything we touched turned to gold. I had long been a great admirer of Gladstone Small in county cricket and wondered why he had never broken through to the England side. It was rumoured that Norman Gifford and David Brown had advised holding him back until he had completed his education on flat Edgbaston wickets and got over a series of injuries; judging by Gladstone's bowling on the Australian tour they were absolutely right to have nursed him. He is similar to Richard Hadlee, and I can think of no higher praise: a short run, a whippy action, a genuine seamer who can also bowl the outswinger. A marvellous serene temperament, nothing seemed to get him down, not dropped catches, nor the racialist baiting from the infamous Bay Thirteen at the Melbourne Cricket Ground. He never seemed to tire in the Australian heat, always wanted to keep going and would do everything asked of him. He was a great tourist and a fine example, and we were all delighted to see him take five wickets in the first innings at Melbourne.

The atmosphere was electric on that first day. The official attendance was 58,000, but with members and guests not included it must have been closer to 70,000, double the biggest crowd I had ever played in front of. The MCG is such a vast place: only when you are out in the middle and you look at the three-tier stands that stretch endlessly round the ground do you appreciate the massive expanse of green, then the huge amphitheatre. As we walked on to the field on that first morning we were swamped by boos and jeers, but that gladiatorial atmosphere only served to inspire us. We wanted to do it for England and we were heartened by the pockets of British support dotted around the auditorium. It was a great occasion in the cricket calendar and we were really fired up to give of our best.

On that first day it was hard to fathom the tactics of the

Australians. The papers had been full of hype from Border, saying that they were going to take the fight to our bowlers and score quickly enough to bowl us out twice. Yet they switched from the first day caution of Adelaide to frenetic suicide. So many of them got out playing reckless shots that it was clear they felt greater pressure than we did. Their team selection was bizarre. We were delighted that Greg Ritchie was left out because we thought he was second only to Border and bound to get a big score soon. John Emburey was beginning to get a mental block about the way Ritchie was messing up his line and he was very pleased to see him out. It meant that Greg Matthews went in at number six, and as he did not bowl one over in the game he was therefore in as a specialist batsman, and on that basis he was one place too high.

Australia effectively lost the game in the first two sessions on the opening day when we bowled them out. After that we had to consolidate on a pitch that was greener than our experienced players could ever remember at the MCG. That did not bother me; I was playing everything on its merits and perfectly happy to go out there and bat for as long as necessary. The first session again went well, as Hughes and the recalled Craig McDermott were keener on fire and brimstone than making us play at the new ball. McDermott was better at vocal abuse than working up any great pace, and once again Bruce Reid was their best bowler.

On the second day I found myself in the history books alongside illustrious names such as Jack Hobbs, Herbert Sutcliffe and Wally Hammond. I made my third hundred in successive Tests and the statisticians had a field day. I was later informed that only Hobbs and Hammond had scored three centuries in successive Tests against Australia, while Sutcliffe was the only other Englishman to score three hundreds in a series in Australia. To be honest, those kind of figures meant little to me because I knew nothing about the respective merits of the bowlers and pitches from yesteryear, but I obviously respected such great names. It is only after retirement that such statistics take on a wider significance, and at the time of my third hundred I was only too aware of my limitations. I really struggled on the second day after my fluent start the evening before; they had to go on the defensive and the fielders plugged the gaps that I had exploited earlier. It was very hard work before lunch and I just hung on. I was dropped in the gully by Steve Waugh, a very sharp chance to his left and I walked away to square leg, chastising myself. I got to lunch 87 not out, grateful that I had survived. Then Mike Gatting was out to the first ball after the interval and I was conscious that I must not get out. I almost seized up in the 90s, scratching around for singles, and when Peter Sleep nearly caught and bowled me at 98 I was very tense. It had by now dawned on me that I was close to the third hundred in a row, and I was far more nervous than at Perth or Adelaide. Allan Lamb was in with me at the time and I remembered that he had made three in a row against the West Indies in 1984, so I sought out his advice. 'Were you more nervous the more times you got a hundred, Lamby?' 'You're joking, of course not. Just get 'em.' 'I can't believe it, I'm ever so nervous now.' That little chat hardly soothed my beating heart, and when I was on 99 I twice refused short singles that I would normally have accepted. Finally, just after 2.30, I managed a little push to mid-wicket off Reid; Sleep misfielded and I was home. I have never done anything as extrovert as a jog on the cricket pitch, but I allowed myself a hop and a skip on my follow-through and turned to the dressing-room to wave at my team-mates. All the windows were open and they were standing up, clapping and waving at me. My parents had gone home – my mascots! – and Carole was *en route* from England, so I just stood there, allowing the emotion to wash all over me. It seemed that all my chickens were coming home happily to roost and laying bumper eggs for me.

Of course I wanted to build on a not-out hundred – I was still greedy! – but Hughes came up with a good one that left me late and I could not avoid touching it to Zoehrer. I had got myself out at Adelaide, but at Perth and Melbourne it was a case of good bowling. As far as the game was concerned the last couple of hours on that second day finished off the Australians. We managed to add another 60 runs for the last two wickets before we were all out to give us a lead of 208. With two innings already completed in just two days it was important to have as big a lead as possible. There seemed little possibility of a draw.

On the third day we could not believe the optimistic tub-thumping from the Australian press. Their scenario was that the Aussies would get around 450, then bowl us out for less than 200 as the pitch deteriorated. Perhaps they had been seduced by the jingoism that attached itself to the Davis Cup tie against Sweden, just along the road at Kooyong. The score was continually flashed up on the giant electronic screen at the MCG, and whenever the Australians – or more specific-ally Pat Cash – won a set, the noise of acclamation was deafening. All this media hype only served to stiffen our resolve. As we read that morning's papers with mounting incredulity, we all agreed that we would get stuck into them and try to finish the job that day. It worked like a dream and it was all over with an hour still to play.

At 113 for 2 they were at least making a fight of it when Gladstone Small produced an excellent piece of tactical intel-ligence. Allan Border had twice thrown the bat at deliveries that screamed through point to the boundary and the crowd gloried in the shots. Gladstone bowled the next one from a foot wider in the crease, changing the angle, and Border flashed at it to be caught at third slip. It may have looked like just another half-volley, but it was rather a case of feeding a batsman's favourite shot and bringing about his downfall with a slight adjustment of line.

When Border was out they just folded. They relied so much on him and no one else seemed keen to prolong things. It reminded me of the way we folded up against the West Indians in 1984; when you are playing badly the feeling seeps in that the luck is also against you, and you lack the will to battle on. We did not spare any sympathy for the Aussies; they would not have wasted a moment thinking about us. Our sights had been set firmly on retaining the Ashes and we had done it in just four Tests after being justifiably written off in the first month of the tour. The Aussies were very down: only Greg Matthews and Allan Border came in for a quick drink and they stayed just a couple of minutes. By now Ian Botham was convinced his great mate would resign the Australian captaincy, and certainly he looked as if he had had a bucketful. The team was too dependent on his batting and I got the impression he was only in charge because there was no one else around to do the job. Yet he hung on, took the flak like a man, and at least got some consolation in the Sydney Test.

Fifteen minutes after we came off the field at Melbourne we were joined in the dressing-room by a euphoric Elton John, and the party was on. After a session at the MCG it was off to Ian Botham's suite in our hotel and a marathon disc jockey's stint from the legend of the rock world. Elton arrived with his silk suit spattered by beer and champagne and told Ian Botham he did not think much of his choice of music. He sent his personal assistant off to his own hotel and he returned with about a hundred compact discs. On request he played just a few of his own, but he soon nipped that in the bud and for the next four hours he stood in front of the compact disc player and organized the music. It was a tremendous party and we were thrilled that a guy of Elton John's stature should be so ecstatic for us.

My delight was of course immense – for myself, for the team, the management and the vast army of supporters who had come over to cheer us on. I also felt happy for the Poms who were living in Australia; from bitter experience in 1979–80 I knew how the Aussies love to rub your nose in it when they are on top, and it was lovely to be able to look them straight in the eye and bring the conversation round to cricket. I loved the headline in a Melbourne paper the day after our victory inside three days: 'Can Pat Cash Play Cricket?' It all meant that fellow professionals like Derek Pringle, Simon Hughes, Graeme Fowler, Paul Terry and Steve Rhodes – who were all playing out there – would get far less abuse than I had faced seven years earlier.

The record books will show that Australia won the Sydney Test, but in all honesty I think we gave it to them. We all wanted to win it, to make it 3–0 for the series, but I am not sure *how* desperately we wanted to come out on top. For my part I was aware of a slackening off in my concentration and attitude; it was not deliberate, just a subconscious feeling that we had already won the series, retained the Ashes and so the important work was over. It was annoying to lose but I think we all agreed it had been a great game of cricket, especially that dramatic final day. For the first time in the series the luck went Australia's way and we cannot really complain about that; but in a match full of imponderables there is no doubt that we were unlucky at crucial times.

On the first morning, Dean Jones had made just 5 when he leg-glanced Gladstone Small into the hands of Jack Richards. We all ran to the keeper to congratulate him on a super catch, only to find that Jones was still there, given not out.

113

We could not believe it. He made another 179 runs in a match we lost by 55 runs when no one else got more than 96. This is not meant to denigrate the umpires: they are only human, after all, and we knew better than anyone about the kind of pressure they were facing. The point about the Dean Jones incident is that he played the crucial innings of the match, yet he did not receive the Man-of-the-Match award. Presumably his luck with that decision told against him with the adjudicators. We all agree that luck with decisions evens itself out over a series and a career, but the Jones decision came at a cruel time. Yet Mike Gatting was quite right to be philosophical about the umpires throughout the tour, and generally I felt we set a good example by refusing to criticize them in public. We all got on with them very well in fact.

If we were unlucky not to get the verdict over Dean Jones, we did not help ourselves when Jack Richards missed an easy stumping in the second innings after Steve Waugh had made just 15. He went on to make another 58 and his stand with Peter Taylor added another 60. That was our fault, even though it was Jack's one real mistake of the series. Another desperately difficult decision went Australia's way on the final evening when we were hanging on for a draw. Gladstone Small was given out, caught by Allan Border at first slip with just fourteen balls to go. The ball was taken low down and Gladstone stood his ground before being given out. Now I am not complaining about the decision because the television playbacks were inconclusive, but Greg Ritchie was the only Australian not to appeal. That was significant because Ritchie was at silly mid-on, standing in direct line to the ball's flight, and he shook his head as everyone else went up. He had done the same at Brisbane when he told Border that a nick by DeFreitas had not carried to slip. I was impressed by Ritchie's honesty, and after the Sydney Test ended he told me that Gladstone was not out. No complaints about the appeal –

we would have been equally positive – and no complaints about the decision, because the umpires have to give it as they see it, without the benefit of electronic aids. It simply underlined that Dame Fortune was going to smile Australia's way for once and she did it with a vengeance.

If John Emburey and Phil Edmonds had not been inconvenienced with bad groin strains, I feel sure they would have dismissed Australia cheaply in the second innings, but they could not swivel properly in their bowling actions and had to rely on putting the ball on the spot, rather than bowling it. Sydney's turn would have been ideal for them if they had been fully fit, and I cannot believe that Australia would then have got to 251 when every run was vital in their second innings. Emburey's groin strain also hampered him as he batted on that final evening. Peter Sleep clean-bowled him with six balls to go, but, if fit, Emburey would not have played back to a ball that shot through low. He would have played forward and probably scampered a single to take the last over – and in those circumstances there are few cooler heads than John Emburey.

Lest all this sounds like the ramblings of a 'whingeing Pom' let me admit that one or two decisions also went our way. Allan Lamb took three catches off bat/pad and not every one looked totally straightforward. David Gower was so certain he was out lbw early on that he almost walked in his first innings: he went on to make a glittering 72. So I suppose it was a case of swings and roundabouts. This time the Aussie selectors got it right by picking Peter Taylor, known to everyone as 'Peter Who?' when he was picked. We were happy enough to see Steve Waugh keep out the impressive all-rounder Simon O'Donnell, and for Greg Ritchie to have to open rather than of Glenn Bishop or Mike Valetta, so we did not give Taylor any thought. Yet he bowled superbly, with a nice loop to his off-spin, lovely flight, a subtle arm ball and the ability to make the ball dip suddenly. Our batters did not treat him with too much respect and as a result he got them out playing attacking shots. I was particularly impressed by the way he stood up to a brief onslaught by Ian Botham in the first innings; a lesser bowler would have fired it in, but he continued to flight it and he got his man. At the age of thirty, Taylor had the maturity to cope with the pressure, as he showed when he batted obdurately in both innings, and those who derided his lack of first-class experience forgot that he had played in grade cricket for years and fared well against many a Test player.

It is a tribute to Mike Gatting's positive leadership that we were still going for victory on that final day, even at 102 for 5, still 218 adrift, and with Peter Taylor on a hat-trick. The loss of Ian Botham first ball was a grievous blow, but the captain was as good as his words of the previous evening. When he was told that England had only once managed to score more than three hundred to win a Test, he said, 'It's about time it was done again, then,' and at no time until the last half-hour did we think of shutting up shop. Gatting played the spinners superbly and with Richards keeping him sensible company the asking rate was down to 90 off 20 overs with 5 wickets left when drinks were taken. In the first over after drinks Gatt was caught and bowled for 96 off Steve Waugh's slower ball. It was a great knock, and even then he was still positive, telling John Emburey, the new batsman, to go for it if he felt it was still there for the taking. When Jack Richards played outside a top-spinner from Sleep it was time to block it out, but at least we had kept going for it longer than any other international teams I could mention.

On that final day I was the only one of the side not directly involved in the action. I had got out the night before in irritating fashion when Sleep bowled me a ball of full length and I toppled over as I played too early, trying to force it through mid-on. I was off-balance, the edge of my bat was turned too much, and I got a leading edge for a comfortable caught and bowled. My concentration lapsed: perhaps I was too relaxed. In the first innings I had the feeling that I had used up all my luck earlier in the series. Merv Hughes bowled me one that pitched middle and off and I shaped to pad up as it was surely going to carry on past off stump; instead it came back very sharply and I was plumb out lbw. My mind went back to the way Joel Garner bowled me at the Oval in 1984 and I came to the conclusion that there was nothing I could have done about it because I had been leaving deliveries like that from Hughes throughout the series and they had passed harmlessly outside the off stump. The wheel of fortune was perhaps moving away from me.

Anyway, the Aussies got their consolation victory and, to judge by their ecstasy, it was as if the events of the past few months had never happened. On the first morning of the Sydney Test their papers were full of gloomy inquests into the state of their cricket; six days later they were hailing this win as one of the greatest in their history. The truth was that we ought at least to have drawn it, might even have won it, and that a margin of 2–1 in the series flattered Australia. It was annoying not to have beaten them by a wider margin and I believe the Australian players knew that 3–0 would have been a fairer reflection. We had made better selections for each Test, they had never got their opening attack right, we were better led and our fielding and catching were superior. It was now time to hammer our superiority home in the one-day matches. We were very determined to ensure there would be no more euphoric days for them like the one we suffered at Sydney.

9

A Clean Sweep in Australia

Our main objective in Australia was to win the Test series and keep the Ashes. To us that was the true test of a side's prowess, rather than in the pressure-cooker atmosphere of limited-overs games. Having said that, we were very keen to triumph in the other two competitions that Australian summer: the Benson and Hedges Perth Challenge and the World Series. To many the Perth Challenge was a spurious contest, designed to maximize interest in the America's Cup, and we did not disagree too vehemently with that assessment. Yet by the time it came around we were perfectly happy to go for the Challenge with all guns blazing. The pressure from the Ashes series had been lifted after our victory in Melbourne and the two free days we had earned put us in high spirits for the trip to Western Australia. We wanted to keep the winning momentum going and we were intrigued to see how we would fare against the Pakistanis and the West Indians, who would join Australia to make it a quartet. The challenge from the West Indies would help us assess how far we had travelled on the road to recovery since the Caribbean horrors

My first Test hundred at Perth – and after seeking out my parents
in the stand, I acknowledge the applause of my team-mates.

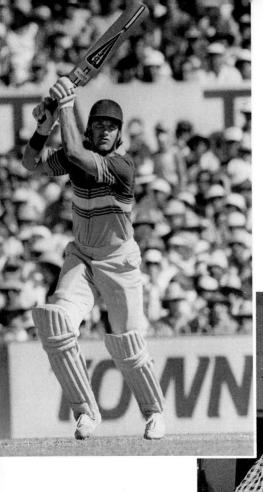

On the way to victory
in the Perth Challenge –
the second instalment of
England's historic treble.

Here I am at the England
touring team's traditional
Christmas Day fancy-dress party.
Look out Lawrence of Arabia!

A moment from my third successive Ashes Test century, at Melbourne –
forcing one past a despairing Allan Border.

The Ashes have been retained after a three-day thrashing of Australia in Melbourne and we are about to embark on a celebration spree that had us roaring for dark glasses and black coffee the following morning.

Opposite above
Elton John, my musical hero for so many years, tries to recover from having celebratory drink poured all over him, while Jack Richards, obscured by the Union Jack, at least has the presence of mind to put a good word in for our bat manufacturer.

Opposite below
The Australian press and commentators often confused which tall, blond Englishman was which while we were out on the field: I suppose I am a marginally better left-hand bat than Graham Dilley!

Applying the long handle during my half century in the World Series Final.

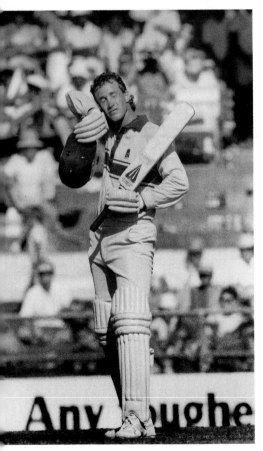

Sydney, February 1987.
We have won the World Series Cup
to complete an unprecedented treble
and Graham Dilley and I are delighted
for our captain, Mike Gatting.
After a moment's hesitation,
we decided against lifting Gatt on to
our shoulders: the English season
was not all that far away!

Taking a breather.

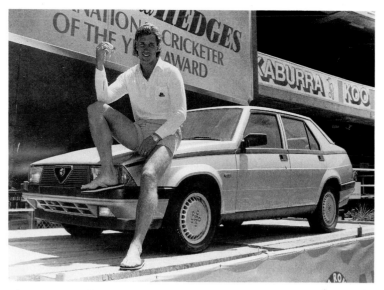

The International Cricketer of the Year for 1986–87 shows off his prize, while wondering if he will ever wake up from such a pleasant dream.

Daddy is finally back from Australia and daughter Gemma is unlikely to let me out of her sight for the next few days.

It was a great pleasure to walk out at Lord's with my Notts colleague Tim Robinson
to open the England innings in the Second Test against Pakistan on 18 June 1987.
I'm told that not since Surrey's Micky Stewart and John Edrich
played against the West Indies in 1963 have two players from the same county
opened the innings for England.

of spring and the anxious summer series against India and New Zealand.

The crucial victory came in our second game when we beat West Indies by 19 runs in an exciting, tense game. It seemed to me that Viv Richards let us off the hook when we were 96 for 5 off 25 of our 50 overs: he kept attacking, maintained his slip fielders, and Allan Lamb and Jack Richards got us up to 228. When they batted they got themselves out through rash shots. They had come from the slow wickets in Pakistan and Sharjah and they were playing too late, whereas we were now used to the extra bounce and the pace of the Perth pitch. They all got out after getting in, and the vital wicket came when Viv Richards lapped John Emburey to me at deep square leg. It came to me out of a dying sun, it was in the air a long time, but I kept my eyes on the ball and held it safely. After that they just folded up, and I was surprised at their lack of pride and fight. Their morale never really improved in either of the limited-overs competitions. They allowed themselves to be rattled by the new regulation about bouncers: the square leg umpire was now empowered to no-ball any delivery that bounced above a batsman's shoulder height, and this rankled with a side that had relied on short-pitched assault for many years. I thought it a justifiable experiment because crowds at the one-day games want to see runs on the board and exciting finishes, rather than batsmen having to duck or fend off systematic short-pitched stuff. It is a much fairer contest if the bowlers have to aim at the stumps, instead of getting away with intimidation, but Viv Richards seemed very down about the regulation and moaned far too much about it. That seeped into the psyche of his team-mates and they seemed to think the whole world was now against them. That was ridiculous – their bowlers were good enough to get anyone out if they put it in the right place on a lively Perth wicket. Viv appeared to lack the confidence in making instant decisions in the hubbub; he was too used to seeing his bowlers knock over a side, and he seemed uneasy in setting a proper field and getting his men to bowl in the proper area. He was far too intolerant of his team-mates, shouting at them if they misfielded. Obviously not having such experience, he seemed to lack the paternal, calming influence of Clive Lloyd and we were very confident of our chances against them after that first encounter in Perth.

So we were in the final, having beaten both Australia and the West Indies. For good measure we beat Pakistan in the third game, then thrashed them in the final. Without Javed Miandad's remarkable 77 not out from a total of 166, it would have been a complete farce, but we won by 5 wickets easily enough with ten overs to spare. Just one incident marred my pleasure and I have to say it was the most incredible decision I have ever suffered. In fact it was so amazing that Dick French, the umpire involved, had a laugh with me about it afterwards and agreed that it was one of those things. We parted friends after he admitted he had simply suffered a complete brainstorm, so that was fair enough. It came when Wasim Akram bowled one around my hip area and I decided not to play at it, allowing the ball to hit the padded area around my hip and then go through to the wicket-keeper. There was an enormous appeal and I walked a few yards towards square leg, as I usually do when I am annoyed at myself for playing a poor shot and to restore my concentration. All the time I was looking at the bowler, shaking my head and laughing at his incredible appeal. Then he appealed a second time. Dick French, leaning forward with his hands on his knees, suddenly stood up straight and raised his finger. I made a gesture that the ball had hit my hip and slouched off, dragging my bat. When I was about twenty yards from the pavilion there was a loud groan from the crowd: they had seen the playback of the incident and gave the umpire a volley of abuse. Mike Gatting replaced me and asked Dick French about the decision, only to be told that he thought I was walking to the dressing-room when I stepped away to square leg. It was all very farcical, but no real harm was done. Not even that decision would warp my judgement against the Aussie umpires: they did their best in trying circumstances and they did not favour any side.

So we had won the Perth Challenge and the prize money was very welcome, even if the Pakistanis scooped more than us because Javed Miandad won a gold watch worth more than £8,000 for being named the Player-of-the-Final. Perth had been a very enjoyable interlude: excellent weather, lavish hospitality, good cricket wickets and the great thrill of playing in night cricket for the first time. Initially I was unsure how I would take to the coloured clothing and all the raz-zamatazz – I am an unashamed traditionalist in these matters – but it helped to be playing with familiar faces in the team and soon I was caught up in the excitement. When the game began there would be very few people in the ground, but it would gradually fill up as work ended, and by the time it was dark the atmosphere was electric. The temperature didn't drop at night and you could sense how much the crowd enjoyed it. It was a sensational sight to look up at a dark sky, then down on to the field of play and take in the bright colours and the white ball. Exhilarating stuff – especially as we kept winning each game.

By the time we came to the World Series finals we were tired and not overjoyed at the prospect of ten more matches, with a few frantic finishes and nerve-jangling incidents thrown in for good measure. Yet we had come out on top already in two contests and we wanted to make it a third. This is where Ian Botham was so influential. He really wanted to make it a clean sweep. After victory in the Brisbane Test he would often say, 'If the Aussies slag you off, just ask them what the score is in the Test series. That'll shut them up.' He had already announced that he would not tour again for England for another three years, so he was to all intents and purposes on his last England trip to Australia. He was desperate to go out on a high note and he dragged us along with him during the World Series games. He pointed out time and again that no team had ever won all three competitions in an Australian season and that it was our chance to make history. It was terrific to hear such commitment from our greatest player and we were all lifted by his example.

We had any amount of hiccups along the way before we beat Australia in the final. We lost three times to Australia, which was infuriating, but when the chips were down we pulled things round. No more so than at Sydney when Allan Lamb hit Bruce Reid for 18 in the last over to give us a desperate win. We did not deserve to win but they panicked; Bruce Reid fumbled a return as Lamby shrewdly got in the way of the bowler and the ball and he scampered another run to give him back the strike. The next ball went to the square leg boundary and we had won, improbably. With 36,000 inside the Sydney Cricket Ground that night, it was an atmosphere I shall not forget.

Yet apart from the night of Lamby's heroics we did keep losing to Australia. After they had thrashed us at Melbourne I went into their dressing-room and slumped down beside Greg Matthews. He said, 'What's going on? Why have you suddenly blown it?' I said we were tired, a little homesick, fed up of travelling – the usual stock excuses. Greg was amazed: 'How can you say that? You'll never be in this position again, with a chance of winning all three competitions.' Those were true words from a great competitor and I communicated Greg's feelings to our lads. Two days later we went out against the West Indies and played superbly to beat them by 29 runs. Ian Botham inspired us by getting rid of Viv Richards with a great ball, and John Emburey finished off the match with three wickets in the final over. It was a terrific team effort as we were defending a smallish total of 177 and it only needed a few overs of magic from Viv to bury us.

So we had made it to the final or, more pertinently, the finals. We were scheduled to play three games: the first at Melbourne, the second at Sydney and the decider at Melbourne if necessary. We did not want there to be an 'if necessary'; we had done enough travelling and the idea of a few days rest in Sydney after the second victory was very seductive. One final heave from everyone was needed, and it was a true example of our wonderful team spirit that we pulled it off. I am convinced that if we had been forced to play the decider in Melbourne we would have lost. We had conditioned ourselves to stay in Sydney and our morale would have suffered severely from another flight.

Ian Botham was at his greatest in both matches. He opened with me at Melbourne in the first game and made a mockery of the contest. I made a poor 12 out of the opening stand of 90, giving the strike to Both, and he thrashed them for 71. We had needed 172 in 44 overs and that ought to have been a difficult task on a greenish wicket, but Botham simply changed the game's complexion. It was fascinating to open with him for the first time. He likes to chat out in the middle – with umpires, opponents and, at the end of every over, his partner. All the while he was boosting my confidence, telling me how well I was playing – it was nonsense but nice to hear! He clearly suffers from nerves when batting, hence the need to keep chattering away, but once he gets his eye in he is almost impossible to bowl at. On this occasion I could see him first build an innings and then cut loose. I have never seen a man hit the ball harder, and at one stage I said to the umpire, Steve Randell, 'If it comes anywhere near me, I'm going behind you!' After that, victory by 6 wickets was a formality.

Three days later came the second of the finals. We just had to win: half of us were carrying strains and I knew I would not be fit to play in a third game. I had been troubled by a strained hamstring for several weeks now and Allan Lamb had the same problem. Dilley, Athey and Gower could not throw for a variety of reasons, so it was a patched-up squad that gathered. Botham again gave us a flying start and I got a fifty, but without some good late-order hitting we would have got a good deal less than 187 for 9. The odds were on Australia, especially when they got to 70 for 1, but then Botham did it again. He was convinced that he had broken a toe while batting but he insisted on bowling out his ten overs. Not only did he do that, not only did he restrict them to a mere 26 runs off those ten overs, but he got the wickets of Border, Marsh and Ritchie. When John Emburey took a spectacular catch off his own bowling to dismiss Jones we were there, barring major mishaps. Botham limped off to a deserved ovation and Gladstone Small came on to perk up the fielding. Dirk Wellham stayed in far too long for Australia's comfort and we were delighted that the dangerous Simon O'Donnell was not pushed up the order. When he eventually came in he showed what could have been possible with some excellent straight hitting, but they were always just short of the target.

We came to the last over with 18 needed and two wickets to fall. O'Donnell was going well and I was worried stiff that he was going to do an Allan Lamb. Neil Foster had to bowl the last over, but he conceded just 9 runs as he sensibly pitched the ball up to the batsmen. It was a strange feeling to know we had won with only two balls still to be delivered; we could not wait to get off the field and share the historic moment with everyone else in the dressing-room. I thought of all the folk back home, shivering amid the snowdrifts, and felt very proud for England as well as ourselves. It was a privilege to be part of the revival and, judging by the messages we were getting from England, our performances were wiping the usual sombre news stories off the front pages of the papers.

We had done it. We had made cricket history. It had been a long haul from the start of October, but terrific team spirit and our professionalism had carried us through. We had got used to the idea of winning, always a happy state of affairs, and I was becoming pleasantly accustomed to winning awards.

10

International Cricketer of the Year

Just before I went out to bat in the Melbourne Test, Ian Botham and John Emburey both said something surprising to me: 'Don't forget the car,' I was told. Now I was busy with my usual pre-innings rituals and I must have looked rather dense at the time: all I was concerned about was getting out there and seeing us through to a big lead. It was only after my third hundred in a row that I could see my way clear to that personal goal. A handsome Alfa Romeo 75 was at stake for the International Cricketer of the Year and I was in the running for it. Perhaps it was an attempt on the part of Botham and Emburey to get my mind attracted by individual rewards, but that was never a factor on the tour. My main concern was for the team to win all three competitions and everything else was just icing on the cake.

Admittedly it was rather delightful icing, and the award was one further example of how much my life has changed in the past year. By the end of the tour I was in danger of laryngitis from a welter of media interviews, both with the Australian version and their counterparts back home. The day after we had won the World Series finals I was live on

TV-AM, talking to Carole and the children, and within a week of my return both Terry Wogan and David Frost had foisted me on a curious nation. It was all very exciting, but I am well aware that producers were only interested in me because I was new to the scene – I made a change from old favourites like Botham and Gower – and because the public could understand what International Cricketer of the Year meant. I took on an agent to take advantage of my new status, but I was well aware that he would have difficulty pushing me in the proper channels unless I kept delivering the goods out on the pitch. I was a nine-day wonder for the media during that marvellous February and I am the only one who can consolidate that heightened public interest. I am not even sure if I want to be all that public. Soon after I got back from Australia, I took Gemma shopping to Grantham and it was a bizarre experience. Before the tour I could have walked down any street in Britain and be recognized by hardly a soul. On this particular Saturday I was conscious that people were nudging each other and pointing at me; to a shy chap like myself it was unsettling. It was the other side of the coin in this new, exciting world I have encountered, and it is up to me to come to terms with it.

This ascent into celebrity status can be such a subtle process. Neil Foster pointed that out to me when we played in Canberra just before Christmas. We were up against the Prime Minister's XI and before the game we were introduced to Bob Hawke, who is a great cricket fan. Mr Hawke shook my hand and had a quick word and moved on. Neil Foster, standing alongside me, whispered: 'Did you get the move-on handshake? I bet you didn't, because you've scored two hundreds in the series already.' As the Prime Minister moved along the line I could see what Neil meant: if he did not want to stand and talk, he would push the proferred hand in the direction of the next player. With the likes of Botham and

127

Gower, he would come to a halt in the same movement as shaking hands. Admittedly a prime minister cannot talk to everyone, but I was now among the elite of the squad because Bob Hawke had exchanged a couple of words with me. Yet it took a colleague not in the Test eleven to bring it to my attention.

A visit to Harold Larwood helped place all the superficialities in perspective. I really enjoyed the morning I spent with him in Sydney and he was fascinating on the players of his era. I had been asked to go and pick up a blazer from Harold for the museum at Trent Bridge and I took Carole with me. I rang the bell and a little old man in carpet slippers came to the door. I had no idea what Harold Larwood looked like and he said, 'I knew I recognized that voice – you're Chris Broad, aren't you?' He brought us indoors and we spent a fascinating morning, looking at his trophies and souvenirs and yarning about life in Nottingham. He clearly missed Trent Bridge and asked after many people. It was such a shame that he could not come over to open the new Larwood and Voce Stand at Trent Bridge, but his eyesight was too poor. Yet his memory was crystal clear and he was only too pleased to pass on some tips about playing in Australia. He showed me the trophy he holds dearest: a silver salver Douglas Jardine gave him at the end of the Bodyline tour, inscribed 'From the Skipper'. Then he gave me something I shall always treasure: a signed copy of his autobiography. He even made his wife check that his signature was legible because he could hardly see any more. It was an immensely rewarding experience to meet a great cricketer who was such a nice, gentle man, and that morning confirmed my view that the players occupy the stage for a time, but that the game is the only enduring thing.

That was one of my outstanding memories of the Australian trip, but there are many more. I did not even mind the travelling, apart from the prospect of another flight to Melbourne in mid-February when we were all out on our feet. Much had been made about the constant shuttling back and forth to opposite ends of Australia, but it was very well organized. We always had a day to recover from a flight, and when we were due to leave for the airport the hotel staff were on hand to look after our luggage so that the inconvenience was minimal. The hotels were good, courtesy cars were mostly available, and we were welcomed with genuine warmth wherever we went. Some of my team-mates were a little world-weary after several tours, but I had no time for that attitude. When I heard them moaning about touring India and Pakistan it only occurred to me that they were very lucky – they could have been stuck in an office at Trent Bridge, hearing how well their county colleagues were doing on tour with England! I do not believe I could ever get blasé about touring with England; it is too exciting and a great honour.

Inevitably I cornered much of the media attention at the end of the tour because of my award, but it was fundamentally a team effort. The management duo of Peter Lush and Micky Stewart worked well because they had clearly defined areas of influence and no grey areas. The captain was very impressive: pugnacious, positive, accessible, he managed to be one of the lads as well as our leader. I really enjoyed my partnerships with Gatt and I liked seeing him come in at number three instead of David Gower. David is such a natural stroke-maker that I would find myself trying to match him and get myself out when my limitations were exposed, but Gatt would fight it out early on and that would inspire me to concentrate and play in the way that suited me. I was surprised to see that David scored more than 400 runs in the Test series, because he never seemed to be in all that long, but once he had sorted himself out in November he looked in a class of his own. He lost his way again after the Tests were over – a combination perhaps of his impending benefit season and a subconscious relaxation after the sterner contests had finished – but he has this great ability to switch on the tap of genius when it is really necessary. I often feel overshadowed when David Gower is on song at the other end, and I have to console myself that it takes all sorts to make a successful batting line-up.

Ian Botham is another who makes it look ridiculously easy and, if he did not fire on every cylinder throughout, he made telling contributions when they were most needed. That Brisbane hundred was very important. It cast a shadow over the Australians for the rest of the tour and they were always wary of his massive influence – look at the number of times Allan Border referred to him in his press conferences. Botham was a marvellous influence at the end of the tour when we were shattered and carrying a lot of injuries. His attitude was genuinely supportive and I remember how thoughtful he was to James Whitaker after he had dropped a horrible skier off Ian's bowling in the first of the World Series finals. James had just come on the field as substitute and Dean Jones hit one miles up in the air; despite a valiant effort, James dropped it at mid-off. Botham went straight to him, put his arm around him and told him to forget it. Many another bowler would have stood there, tearing out his hair and cursing the fielder, but Botham was big enough to imagine how poor James must have felt.

As vice-captain, John Emburey was a constant source of common sense. He has a great cricket brain and I do not think he will be totally fulfilled until he captains a county side. I was surprised that Surrey did not ask him to be their new captain for 1987. He has much to offer, yet I found it strange that a bowler of his class should get so uptight about his rhythm, or a strong cross-wind, or the way batsmen like

Greg Ritchie could mess up his line. Embers has so many gifts that it should be the batters who ought to do the worrying, but he has a strange insecurity that manifests itself in his desire to bowl a lot of maidens. He likes to be economical in preference to taking wickets at a higher cost. Phil Edmonds is temperamentally different and he is more dangerous on a turning wicket because he accepts that someone will try to get after him. He is willing to gamble runs for wickets and invariably does better than Embers when the ball is turning sharply. As a partnership we were lucky to have them. The left-arm/right-arm combination brought variety and their great experience was invaluable at Adelaide (when we needed to keep the run rate down) and at Melbourne (when inexperienced batsmen panicked in the second innings against the turning ball). It must have been a great consolation to Mike Gatting to know that if his seamers could not break through he had two high-class spinners on hand to do whatever job was necessary.

Our seam bowlers made great advances on the tour. Graham Dilley convinced me that he will remain at the top of the ladder for some time, as long as he can maintain fitness. His technique is now more varied and he bowls the deliveries that get the best batsmen out. He is still not a very confident character – he gets depressed when chances are missed off his bowling – but I am sure that his Australian success and Botham's chivvying at Worcester will make him mentally tougher. Phillip DeFreitas bowled superbly, apart from a period in January when he looked very tired. He was not really expected to play in the early Tests but he looked the best of the seamers in the first month and he deserved his selection. He was an ideal partner to Dilley, with the senior partner capable of late swing and DeFreitas hitting the seam regularly. Phillip does not swing the ball all that much – perhaps Ken Higgs, his coach at Leicester, should teach him

131

a thing or two about shining the ball – but he uses the seam intelligently and is a good deal quicker than he looks. Nobody bowled better than he did in the World Series finals and I think he could be a terrific bowler in a year or so. He has to work at his batting if he wants to be a genuine all-rounder – he tried to work the ball to leg far too often – but he has the natural timing if he can tighten up his technique. As for Gladstone Small, the highest praise I can offer is that he reminded me of Richard Hadlee. We also had Neil Foster on hand, a man good enough to take a hundred wickets in the 1986 season, the only Englishman to do so. He was admirably steady when it was crucial, as it was during the last over of the tour when Simon O'Donnell threatened to take us to Melbourne for the tie-breaker.

As for B. C. Broad, I cannot complain about a Test average of 69.57, the Man-of-the-Series award and a car as the prize for being International Cricketer of the Year. In fact I am still staggered at the way the tour went for me. I must point out that the Australian bowling was not fearsome. Among their opening bowlers, Hughes loved to bang the ball into the middle of the pitch, Lawson and McDermott looked unfit and listless, Chris Matthews was too inexperienced, Mike Whitney did nothing with the ball, while Bruce Reid did not swing it in the air and bowled mainly into the left-hander, allowing me to take the ball on the pads or body a lot of the time. If Reid could develop the one that dips in to the right-hander he would be a terrific bowler, rather than a highly respected one who would be an excellent support to a Lillee or a Hogg. Their spinners were not impressive either, several rungs below Edmonds and Emburey in class. Peter Taylor looked the best and he only had one Test to show what he could do. In contrast to our fielding they looked rather lack-lustre, despite the constant hand-clapping and soccer-style clenching of fists. In short, it was not a vintage Australian side, and their bowling and out-cricket simply did not compare with the team that I faced on my Test début in 1984.

Yet they cannot take my runs away from me. I had waited a long time to prove myself with England and I felt that the experience I picked up in Australia would be invaluable for sterner struggles. My father was rather pleased with the tour as well. When I told him about joining Hobbs and Hammond after my Melbourne hundred, he said, 'Hobbs I admired greatly, Hammond I watched for years at Bristol, and Chris Broad's my son.' I think he enjoyed that statistic.

11

Thoughts on Batting

As I reeled off the hundreds in Australia, many asked me if I had changed my technique, as if sudden success is due entirely to technical alterations. No, the Chris Broad that batted in Australia is the same model that has seen duty for the past five years, even down to the jutting backside that caused so much amusement when I first played for England. I admit my stance is far from classical, but it feels comfortable to me and that is the most important consideration. I think the jutting backside was accentuated against the West Indies because I was more tense than in later years: inevitably I was more crouched in 1984 because the bowling was faster and more intimidatory, whereas in Australia I could stand up a little more against bowling that was never more than fast medium.

In common with most left-handers I have come to terms with being beaten regularly outside the off stump. I am aware that left-handers have the reputation of being a shade loose because we seem to dart a lot at the ball on or near our off stump, but it is often forgotten that it stems from the line on which the bowler is attacking. There are very few left-arm opening bowlers in county cricket – perhaps that is why we struggled against the breed in Australia early on – and we usually face a bowler coming right arm over the wicket. Invariably the line of delivery means that we get passed on the off side a lot because the natural swing of the delivery is taking the ball away from the left-hander's off stump. It is simply a case of getting used to the moans from the bowler and hoping you miss the ball by a long way. When I was a lad I noticed that batsmen like Bill Lawry and John Edrich were often beaten outside the off stump yet piled up big scores, and their phlegmatic attitude was the right one.

At some stage every batsman gets a little ruffled by fast bowlers but so far they have not worried me physically. I have never felt physical fear – possibly because I have played a lot of contact sports like rugby and hockey – and the mind has a lot to do with that. If you think you are going to be hit, you will get injured at some stage because the mind influences the physical reactions. That is why I never like to get ready to bat too early; I do not want to think who will be bowling because then I shall start to wonder what is in store. After careful preparation I just like to pick up my bat and be off out of the door. In contrast, Tim Robinson – a more punctilious man than I – is always ready a few minutes early, then collects himself quietly. It is sad to see how some players react to the quicks when their nerve has gone: Derek Randall, for one, never looks happy any more against high pace, and Tim Robinson went through a bad patch in 1986. In my first year in county cricket Glamorgan's Mike Llewellyn kept turning his back on Mike Procter's deliveries, letting them hit him, or backing away. There is very little you can do when the mind starts influencing the way you play the fast bowlers. I just hope I can continue enjoying the challenge they represent.

Having started as a middle-order batsman in county

cricket, it would be wrong to say that I was fated to do battle with the quicks. It simply evolved after a couple of seasons when it became clear that a player who did not seem unduly troubled by them should move up the order and open. I suppose my excellent eyesight helps; when we were in Perth, Carole was astonished that I could see the scoreboard at the ground from our hotel room, half a mile away! You have to make up your mind fairly swiftly when the ball is on its way at high speed, so fast reactions stemming from good eyesight are a considerable help.

I never consciously stiffen my stance until the ball is about to be delivered. Before then it is important to be as relaxed as possible. I once noticed that in Viv Richards: he looked very casual until the bowler arched his back, then he tensed up. So I steel myself to grip the bat tight only when I am about to hit the ball. I figure that such preparation will suit me if the world's greatest batsman approaches the job in the same way. As the bowler turns in his run-up, I like to settle in my stance and watch him run all the way in. That helps turn off my mind to anything else. Norman Gifford has always been a problem to batsmen in that respect: the wily old boy knows that batsmen like their routine and he will try to unsettle us by turning quickly and running in to bowl before we are completely ready. In those circumstances the best thing to do is to stand aside, apologize for not being ready and prepare for a blast from Norman!

Against fast bowling I stand outside the crease. I used to straddle the crease, but found I was not getting forward enough and was getting out lbw on pitches of low bounce. I wanted to feel I was rocking back and forth, to get my momentum going, so I needed to be in a good position if I was forced back by a short-pitched delivery. As the ball is being delivered, my weight is ready to be transferred either on to the front or the back foot, and if I do have to go back

I am still a fair way from my stumps because I am outside the crease line. My long reach also enables me to play a long way forward, so the risk of an lbw is minimized. I changed to this area of stance when I came to Trent Bridge in 1984 because I knew that I would face extra bounce compared to Bristol, and it has helped me. Two years earlier I had decided to stand with my bat raised while the bowler ran in to deliver. In my early days with Gloucestershire I would stand still and wait for the ball to be delivered before I moved, but I found that the ball was on me too soon. Graham Wiltshire, our coach, said I was right to stand still because I was a front-foot player and should be ready to go forward at the last instant from a rigid position. Yet I noticed that front-foot players like Dennis Amiss and Graham Gooch were now raising their bats before delivery, so that was good enough for me. When I did my advanced coaching course at Bisham Abbey I was told by the National Cricket Association coach, Les Lenham, that I ought to encourage my young pupils to get the bat up early. Clearly that was now official NCA policy, and I believed I had to be consistent in my coaching and my own batting, so I have stuck to the raised bat ever since. I was just too relaxed for too long when the bat was on the ground and now I feel comfortable, but more ready to react.

I use a bat that weighs around three pounds, and my manufacturer, Duncan Fearnley, ensures the weight is close to the bottom of the bat, in the drive area. As a predominantly front-foot player I need to feel that my most productive shots will be favoured! I am not a naturally free hitter but I think I have at last come to terms with that. I have thought an awful lot about how I could improve my batting if I could play shots like a Gower or a Botham, but it seems to me that my job is to blunt the opening attack and make it easier for the stroke-players. My task is to keep the score ticking over, give the strike to anyone who fancies taking an attack apart, and continue accumulating whenever possible. This is most important in limited-overs cricket, where a good start is vital. Too often panic sets in if the scoring rate is a little tardy early on; it is infinitely preferable to have wickets in hand in the second half of the innings so that the dashers can then attack, rather than face a rebuilding job after fifteen overs or so. In such circumstances I can do more for my side out there in the middle, going up a gear or two and supporting the big hitter. Nothing annoys a bowler more than those little edges and nudges that race away to the boundary, particularly at the start of an innings when they are looking to pick up a wicket or two with the new ball. I used to worry about hitting out to get me out of a rut – particularly when the slow bowlers were tying me down – but now I realize that the best bowlers can deliver bad balls and I have to wait for them. That worked like a dream in Australia because every now and then the spinners would lose concentration and give me something to put away. Such pickings are few and far between against the likes of Emburey, Edmonds and Gifford, but I shall just have to get used to grafting away against the spinners and not get too worried if I am scoring slowly. I cannot score runs back in the dressing-room and if my team needs me to stay out there, so be it. It would be lovely to play like I did during my 162 at Perth – even down to the absence of sharp singles! – but it is obvious that such days will happen only occasionally for someone of my limitations. It is up to me to ensure I just keep doing myself justice and leave the fireworks to others more suited to dazzling strokeplay.

Concentration is one facet of batting that now comes very easily to me. I like to chat to the umpire or fielders at the bowler's end to release the tension, and I love to look around, taking in the scenery or spotting friends in the crowd, but the scales really come down when I take guard. One example of this came at Melbourne when I scored my third Test hundred in a row. Merv Hughes was storming in to bowl at me on the first evening when I pulled away. Many thought it was because of a massive roar from the crowd as the Davis Cup score was flashed up on the electronic scoreboard, but not so. I simply wanted to stop some spectators from moving around behind the bowler's arm. The latest news of Pat Cash's heroics that excited around 70,000 at the MCG was a complete irrelevance to me; I was utterly unaware of the hubbub.

When I lose the knack of concentration and my reactions slow up, I shall have to consider dropping down the order. When I played for Orange Free State I batted at number five to stiffen up a weak batting side, and it was quite enjoyable, but I would never want to stay there while everything was in full working order. I really enjoy the challenge of fast bowling, the raw edge of tension, the battle against speed. For me there is no place like the top of the order.

12

The 'Nearly Men' of County Cricket

When I moved to Trent Bridge in 1984 I was far more optimistic about winning domestic honours than playing for England. My ambitions to play Test cricket were no greater than any other professional player, even if some sections of the press chose to represent my move as 'Broad goes to Nottingham to play for England'. At that stage in my career I did not feel I was good enough to play for my country, but I was sure that I would enjoy my cricket more if I played for a team that appeared to be going places. The irony is that Nottinghamshire has missed out on every honour since my move, while I have surprised myself and many others by prospering in the England side.

It frustrates all of us at Trent Bridge that we have won just the 1981 County Championship in a decade full of great individual achievements and impressive teamwork. This has been a period when we have had six England players on our books – Broad, Robinson, Randall, French, Hemmings and Hendrick – plus two great international all-rounders in Rice and Hadlee and, in Paul Johnson, a young batsman destined to play for England. Of course we have had our agonizing near-misses, but how could we not win the 1984 Championship when Richard Hadlee became the first player to do the Double since 1967? These days any bowler who gets a hundred wickets in a season is a match-winner, and Richard has been the world's outstanding new-ball bowler for most of the 1980s. Yet we keep missing out: runners-up in two Lord's finals, the same in the Championship, plus two fourth places, a second and a third in the Sunday League, and twice losing semi-finalists in the Benson and Hedges Cup. Why?

I am afraid the buck has to stop somewhere. Clive Rice is very much his own man and his captaincy methods worked in 1981, but since then we have failed with arguably a better squad of players than in the championship year. I am a great admirer of Clive's commitment to Nottinghamshire over the years, and he reminds me a lot of his fellow South African, Mike Procter. Yet Clive does not seem to have been fully tuned in to our cricket at times in recent seasons – understandable when you consider he had a benefit season in 1985 and he clearly has to work out where his domestic future lies as his career comes to an end. Perhaps that is why we have occasionally drifted on the field. Clive's eventual departure will leave a considerable void, not least of all because his all-round skills made him a captain who lead by personal example.

Yet Clive should be around at the start of pre-season training, not only to boost morale but also to sort out any niggles. An occasional source of irritation in our dressing-room is the fact that we have been on the same bonus system since 1980. It came to a head in 1984 when we finished second in the John Player League but only picked up three bonus payments for the whole season. This was because we were only entitled to a bonus if we were in the top four, but for most of that season we were not in that group. We came storming through at the end of the season to finish second, yet we had little in our pockets to show for it. Now this might appear petty but such matters can drag on and get out of proportion. It must be admitted that the club pay us a good basic salary and that they look after us when it comes to organizing sponsored cars, but the bonus issue has been a problem. Perhaps the crucial point is that an overseas captain should do more than arrive late in April and leave for home in mid-September. They should be around for key decisions by committees that affect the players and represent our interests.

As overseas players go, Nottinghamshire has been incredibly lucky with Clive Rice and Richard Hadlee. They have given terrific value and deserve whatever contracts the club has offered. Some counties never seem to get the overseas player equation right, but we have done so and their departure will leave two massive holes in our playing resources. I do not think Richard and Clive are as close as they once were, possibly because Clive has been left behind statistically, as Richard continues to turn in great all-round performances. Clive remains a very fine batsman but injuries hampered his bowling in recent years, and there was always the understandable frustration of not being able to play Test cricket. Richard has also felt the anguish of not winning English trophies. He could have signed for Essex in the late 1970s and I often wonder if he regrets the decision. He is too much of a proud professional to say so, but all those near-misses must have been galling to him. We ought to have supported him better, especially in 1984. Time and again he has decimated the top order and we have not capitalized. In the past Richard would get very down about that, and about dropped catches off his bowling, and his ultra-professional attitude would often rub up some of our team-mates the wrong way. I have never blamed him for that: it is tremendous that a man of his world-class gifts should still possess such high standards. Perhaps Richard has had trouble accepting that others lack his great ability, although he has got a little more philosophical in the last couple of seasons. He sets a marvellous example and it does not bother me at all that he is money conscious; whenever we have been near a trophy, he would say, 'Come on lads, it's an extra grand if we do it,' rather than talking about the achievement in itself. Richard is entitled to gee himself up in whatever way he chooses because he has given us so much.

Richard Hadlee was one of the main reasons why I joined Nottinghamshire in preference to other counties. I have always admired him immensely and playing alongside him has increased that admiration. I consider him the best all-rounder in the world. I know that may stagger Ian Botham's supporters – after all Botham is the better batsman and superior all-round fielder. But Hadlee often takes some great catches at slip, even if he also drops some easy ones, and he is a very dangerous, clean-hitting batsman. Not in the same class as Botham the batsman, I agree, but the gulf is even greater when you consider their bowling. Hadlee is the greatest in the world for my money. Unlike the great West Indian bowlers, he has usually lacked support at the other end and has had to rely on fitness and mental courage to keep going. Apart from Michael Holding no one in my time has approached his beautiful action from an economical run-up. Many fast bowlers rely on physical momentum and sheer running power to generate speed but Richard gets it through timing, with the wrist cocked to release the ball at just the right moment. This gift of timing is as important to a fast bowler as a batsman, and that is why such a slim man as Hadlee can generate surprising pace and lift from such a short run-up.

The Trent Bridge wicket over the years has favoured Richard but it is the same for the opposition, and he also gets plenty of wickets away from home. In any event, Trent Bridge has lost a bit of pace in recent seasons, and the bounce has become rather inconsistent. Too often we have found ourselves trying to bowl out the opposition on a flat wicket on the last day, with snicks off the spinners not carrying to the slips like they used to in the early 1980s. The most damning statistic about recent Trent Bridge seasons came in 1985, when we managed to win just one Championship game at home. There were too many draws, some of them frustrating ones.

In my time there we have never lacked talent. Inconsistent, yes, but never dull. I suppose Derek Randall epitomizes our cricket. Some seasons you think he is on the way out, then he bounces back and delights us all over again. In 1985 all sorts of rumours were flying around that Derek was going to retire, that he had lost his appetite for the fray, particularly against fast bowling. Certainly he was very downcast after being dropped by England after the Edgbaston massacre in 1984. He was placed at number three against the West Indian quicks and predictably he looked awful, making one in two innings. It means so much to Derek Randall to play for England that he has never complained about batting in any position, yet he was clearly ill-equipped technically to go out and face the new ball. Derek has a little twitch and movement towards square leg just as the fast bowler delivers the ball and it is true that he does not look all that comfortable against high speed. Yet he is very difficult indeed to set a field to: he steps back and smashes it through the covers, or flat-bats it past point, or plays a ridiculous shot over mid-wicket when the ball is on middle and off. Derek would have murdered the Indian bowlers on flat wickets out there in 1984–5, but it was not to be. He has not played for England since that Edgbaston Test, and I was beginning to wonder how long he would stay in the game when he suddenly found his form in 1985 and made over 2,000 runs. He was a revelation; he started off well and just kept going, murdering the spinners and medium-pacers and getting out of the way when the quicks bounced him. We were absolutely delighted, because Derek is a much-loved, genuine eccentric who always cheers us up. When he gets down, he is very down and life is simply happier when he is his usual extrovert, dotty self.

I think our management have been absolutely right to give Derek his head and let him go his own sweet way. He is a supreme individualist, a crowd-pleaser who communicates his enjoyment of the game to the public and they rightly love him for it. Even when he is dismissed, he will not moan about it on the way back to the pavilion. Only after he has uttered some wisecrack and given a smile to the members while walking up the stairs will he curse in the privacy of the dressing-room. Derek knows that the public do not wish to see his darker side and he is right; they love him and he will not disappoint. Mind you, he can be exasperating in the dressing-room. He is the untidiest cricketer I have known. Try as he might he cannot collect all his gear and put it in one place. He is also the quickest changer I have seen. He parks his car as close to the gates as possible and on some days, if Tim and I are opening the batting late on, he will have gone by the time we get into the dressing-room at close of play. If he gets out early Derek will change into his civvies, nip into town for a haircut or go home for an hour to have a cup of coffee with his family. Always coffee: Derek drinks it all day.

For such an eccentric batsman he is a very dedicated practiser. If there are no net facilities he will happily bat against a bowling machine for ages, and hit hundreds of balls to perfect a specific stroke. At this stage in his career you would imagine that he has more or less sorted out how to play a particular stroke, but Derek just loves to bat. Perhaps it gives him something to do, because he is incapable of sitting still!

I have no idea what Derek will do when he retires. I cannot see him in a nine to five job, shuffling paperwork, but he is unlikely to be taken seriously enough to coach adults. He is marvellous with kids; they idolize him because he is so much fun, and it may be that he will take to coaching youngsters. Whatever he chooses to do, he will not stray far from home. Touring abroad was hard on a man who lives for his family and he will be happy to be finished with all that now that his own kids are growing up. He even calls his young son 'Rags' (one of Derek's more printable nicknames!) and it is lovely to see him trying to encourage the lad to be as exuberant as his dad. I am sure his wife Liz will organize him once he retires, and when he does I hope everyone will acknowledge that we will have lost a supreme entertainer, a man loved throughout the cricket world for his exuberance and zaniness.

Bruce French is another individualist in our dressing-room. Vegetarian, real-ale enthusiast and inveterate rock-climber, Bruce is not a man who conforms to the stereotypes, but he is an excellent wicket-keeper. When I came to Trent Bridge I thought that Gloucestershire's Jack Russell was the best around, but Bruce looked brilliant after he came back from the Indian tour. In 1985 he was rather inconsistent and he was depressed after the West Indies tour in 1986, feeling that he would never get a chance of playing for England, with no higher prospect than a reliable number two. As soon as he was picked to play at Lord's against India he was back to his very best form, and he showed what he could do when he came in for the last matches in Australia. Perhaps Bruce should share his problems with his team-mates because he keeps himself very buttoned up, as you would expect from someone so keen on a solitary hobby like rock-climbing. If he had the dedication of Jack Richards, Bruce would be an automatic selection for England and I think that has now got home to him. He knows that Jack leapt ahead of him because of superior batting and Bruce is now determined to get 1,000 runs a season. He could do it as well. In the nets he plays all the shots, but he chooses the wrong time when he is out in the middle. We often joke that he needs to be hit by a fast bowler to make him mad, to force him to get in line and battle away. He concentrates with the gloves on, so why does he not do the same when batting? I believe that he is potentially as good a batsman as Jack Richards, and it is about time Bruce scored consistent runs. If he does, he will score them with a flourish and a flamboyant sweep of the bat: Bruce is not a nudger, as he proved with that spectacular half century against Pakistan in the 1987 Old Trafford Test.

So Bruce has much to play for in the next year or so. The same applies to Chris Broad and Tim Robinson. We would dearly love to be the regular England opening pair as well as the Notts openers. Many hurdles still have to be cleared before that ever comes to fruition, one of which is that Graham Gooch is the outstanding English opener of our generation. Perhaps Graham might one day decide to drop down the order and settle for crashing tired bowlers around who have to make do with an old ball? Lord knows, he has the shots to make hundreds of runs at speed. Tim and I have such a competitive streak that I feel sure that an international partnership would be good for us. Each of us loves to outlast the other at the crease and we are the types who thrive on a challenge. The next challenge is to be recognized as the best opening pair in county cricket. I still think that Geoff Cook and Wayne Larkins of Northants are ahead of us because of their consistency over the past decade. Great runners between the wickets, with contrasting styles, they are highly respected in the game. It is up to us to maintain similar consistency over the next few years. That is the only way you get picked for England, either as individuals or as a pair.

Tim and I are equally keen on captaining Nottinghamshire. At the moment Tim is ahead of me as he is the vice-captain, being presumably groomed to take over from Clive Rice. I know that our cricket manager Ken Taylor has strong views about England players captaining county sides – he considers that they do not give of their best with Test distractions. Yet I feel Tim still has much to offer England, especially if he can get back to his majestic form of 1985.

Whoever is the future captain, he will have to inject greater consistency into the side. We owe it to the Nottinghamshire public who have seen us come so close far too often. We must win something for them before the 1980s are dismissed as the 'if only' years at Trent Bridge. I want to win trophies for the supporters as much as for myself. Carole and I were made so welcome when we came up to Nottingham after the traumas at Bristol, and I have built up a fantastic rapport with the regular cricket followers. It is a marvellous atmosphere at Trent Bridge, a ground with a sense of history that impresses even modern professionals who could not name one of those whiskery characters who stare out at us from faded team photographs on the walls on the staircase and in the bars. It is about time the current wearers of the Notts sweaters did something that will be remembered for years to come. Then my cup of happiness really would run over.